Exchange Rate Movements and Their Impact on Trade and Investment in the APEC Region

Takatoshi Ito, Peter Isard,
Steven Symansky, and Tamim Bayoumi

INTERNATIONAL MONETARY FUND
Washington DC
December 1996

Library of Congress Cataloging-in-Publication Data

Exchange rate movements and their impact on trade and investment in the
    APEC region / Takatoshi Itō . . . [et al.].
        p.   cm. — (Occasional paper ; 145)
    Includes bibliographic references.
    ISBN 1-55775-600-7
    1. Foreign exchange — Asia.   2. Foreign exchange — Pacific Area.
    3. Capital movements — Asia.   4. Capital movements — Pacific Area.
    5. Asia — Commerce.   6. Pacific Area — Commerce.
    I. Itō, Takatoshi, 1950– .   II. Series: Occasional paper (International
    Monetary Fund) ; no. 145.
    HG3968.E94   1996   96-39240
    332.4'56'095—dc21   CIP

Price: US$15.00
(US$12.00 to full-time faculty members and
students at universities and colleges)

Please send orders to:
International Monetary Fund, Publication Services
700 19th Street, N.W., Washington, D.C. 20431, U.S.A.
Tel.: (202) 623-7430   Telefax: (202) 623-7201
Internet: publications@imf.org

recycled paper

Contents

Tables

Figures

The following symbols have been used throughout this paper:

. . .   to indicate that data are not available;

—   to indicate that the figure is zero or less than half the final digit shown, or that the item does not exist;

–   between years or months (for example, 1991–92 or January–June) to indicate the years or months covered, including the beginning and ending years or months;

/   between years (for example, 1991/92) to indicate a crop or fiscal (financial) year.

"Billion" means a thousand million.

Minor discrepancies between constituent figures and totals are due to rounding.

The term "country," as used in this paper, does not in all cases refer to a territorial entity that is a state as understood by international law and practice; the term also covers some territorial entities that are not states, but for which statistical data are maintained and provided internationally on a separate and independent basis.

Glossary

APEC	Asia-Pacific Economic Cooperation Council (members: Australia, Brunei Darussalam, Canada, Chile, China, Hong Kong, Indonesia, Japan, Korea, Malaysia, Mexico, New Zealand, Papua New Guinea, the Philippines, Singapore, Taiwan Province of China, Thailand, and the United States)
FDI	Foreign direct investment
ICP	International Comparison Project (United Nations)
NIEs	Newly industrializing Asian economies (Hong Kong, Korea, Singapore, and Taiwan Province of China)
OECD	Organization for Economic Cooperation and Development
PPP	Purchasing power parity
SNA	*System of National Accounts* (European Union, International Monetary Fund, Organization for Economic Cooperation and Development, United Nations, and World Bank, 1993, *System of National Accounts 1993* (Brussels/Luxembourg, New York, Paris, and Washington))

Preface

This Occasional Paper contains an overview followed by three sections analyzing exchange rate movements and their impact on trade and investment in the Asia-Pacific Economic Cooperation Council (APEC) region. The three analytical sections were prepared by the Economic Modeling and External Adjustment Division of the Research Department, headed by Peter Isard, in response to a request made by the APEC ministers of finance. Steven Symansky and Tamim Bayoumi were also extensively involved in the preparation of the sections, and significant contributions were made by Leonardo Bartolini and Michael Klein. Takatoshi Ito, coauthor of the overview section, supervised the study and presented it to the Working Group of APEC Finance Ministers and Central Bank Governors in September 1995, and at the APEC Finance and Central Bank Deputies Meeting in October. The study was given further consideration by the finance and central bank deputies in February 1996, and a summary was presented to the finance ministers and central bank governors in March.

The authors received helpful comments from their colleagues in the Research Department and from staff in other IMF departments. They are grateful to Susanna Mursula for research assistance and to Norma Alvarado and Helen Hwang for secretarial assistance. James McEuen of the External Relations Department edited the manuscript and coordinated production of the publication.

The opinions expressed in the study are those of the authors and do not necessarily reflect the views of the IMF or its Executive Directors.

1 Overview

Takatoshi Ito and Peter Isard

The 18 members of the Asia-Pacific Economic Cooperation Council (APEC) encompass both a wide geographic area and extensive differences in stages of economic development. At the same time, most of the APEC region has experienced a dynamic process of economic development over the past decade, driven to a considerable degree by trade liberalization and economic reforms.

The diverse stages of development of APEC members, and the rapid growth rates of many of them, are summarized in Table 1-1 (Brunei Darussalam has been excluded from this study because data are not readily available). The wide range of income levels may be noted from the first column of the table; for example, the four least developed members of APEC have per capita incomes no greater than 5 percent of the levels prevailing in the United States and Japan, the two most industrialized members. The relatively rapid growth rates of many APEC members, which are among the fastest-growing economies in the world, can be seen in the second column: 10 of the 17 APEC economies studied enjoyed average annual growth rates in excess of 3 percent over the 1983–93 decade; for six of these economies, growth rates have exceeded 5 percent. Such rapid growth has been facilitated by high levels of investment and trade and has given rise to extensive changes in industrial structures and international linkages. Moreover, in most APEC economies, macroeconomic policies have succeeded in sustaining impressive rates of growth without inducing excessive inflation.

The wide-ranging levels of economic development and rapid rates of growth of the APEC members make them an attractive sample on which to base a study of medium- to long-term movements in real exchange rates and the impact of exchange rate changes on trade and investment. This Occasional Paper presents studies of three aspects of these topics. Section II focuses on long-run movements in real exchange rates; Section III considers international trade and real exchange rates in the APEC region; and Section IV examines foreign direct investment (FDI) and its relationship to exchange rates in the region.[1] A summary of these three sections follows.

Long-Run Movements in Real Exchange Rates

Although it is extremely difficult to predict or explain short-run movements in exchange rates, there is strong evidence that long-run movements in nominal exchange rates can be explained to a very significant extent by inflation differentials. There is only a limited understanding, however, of the substantial changes over the long run that many countries have experienced in their real exchange rates, defined as nominal exchange rates adjusted by relative national price levels. Particular interest has been attracted by the substantial real appreciation of the Japanese yen against the U.S. dollar over the past four decades, both before and after the shift from a fixed to a floating nominal exchange rate regime in the early 1970s.[2]

The usual explanation for the real appreciation of the yen is the so-called Balassa-Samuelson hypothesis. Simply put, this hypothesis states that relatively rapid output growth tends to be associated with more rapid productivity growth in the tradable goods sector than in the nontradables sector, putting upward pressure on the price of nontradables relative to the price of tradables. Under conditions in which the relative price of tradable goods across countries remains approximately constant, such a rise in the relative price of nontradables would lead in turn to real exchange rate appreciation.

---

[1]Various issues related to international portfolio investment and surges in capital inflows have been addressed in previous studies prepared for the APEC finance ministers by IMF staff; see Mohsin S. Khan and Carmen M. Reinhart, eds., 1995, *Capital Flows in the APEC Region*, Occasional Paper 122 (Washington: International Monetary Fund).

[2]The real appreciation of the yen against the dollar (based on GDP deflators as measures of national price levels) averaged nearly 1¾ percent a year during the 1955–70 period and more than 3 percent a year during 1973–95.

Table 1-1. Per Capita GDP of APEC Members

Member[1]	Per Capita GDP[2]	
	Level in 1993	Growth rate, 1983–93 (in percent a year)
Australia	16,776	1.9
Canada	20,041	1.1
Chile	2,434	4.8
China	341	8.6
Hong Kong	13,664	5.4
Indonesia	621	4.2
Japan	24,916	3.2
Korea	6,398	7.6
Malaysia	2,559	3.8
Mexico	2,915	–0.0
New Zealand	12,711	0.5
Papua New Guinea	936	2.3
Philippines	701	–1.3
Singapore	14,481	5.1
Taiwan Province of China[3]	8,374	6.0[4]
Thailand	1,631	6.9
United States	21,605	1.8

[1]Excluding Brunei Darussalam.

[2]Per capita GDP measures represent national accounts data converted at 1990 exchange rates into constant (1990) U.S. dollars.

[3]This study follows the IMF convention of using the name Taiwan Province of China to refer to the economy called Chinese Taipei on the official APEC membership list.

[4]1981–91.

The question whether rapid output growth tends to be associated with real exchange rate appreciation in general—that is, whether Japan's experience extends to other economies—has been an important topic of investigation in conceptual and empirical research on the long-run behavior of exchange rates. Section II addresses this question for the APEC region. The relationship between changes in real exchange rates and per capita GDP for fast-growing APEC economies shows a wide range of experiences over the past two decades (see Figure 2-5). Like Japan, Korea and Taiwan Province of China have shown strong positive correlations between per capita growth and real exchange rate changes. By contrast, Hong Kong, Singapore, and Thailand have experienced high economic growth rates with virtually constant real exchange rates; Indonesia and Malaysia have experienced high growth rates with moderate real depreciations; and China has exhibited rapid growth accompanied by a large real depreciation.

These different combinations of growth and real exchange rate outcomes appear puzzling, but the puzzle can be resolved in terms of two different phenomena. First, the experiences of several APEC economies do not conform to the hypothesis that rapid output growth is associated with an upward trend in the relative price of nontradables to tradables. In particular, while the experiences of most APEC members since the early 1970s are consistent with a positively sloped relationship between the change in the relative price of nontradables and the growth rate of per capita GDP, for Singapore, Malaysia, Thailand, and Indonesia rapid output growth has not been associated with an increase in the relative price of nontradables (see Figure 2-6).[3]

A second reason that relatively rapid output growth has not always been associated with real exchange rate appreciation is that the relative prices of tradable goods across countries have not been constant over time but, rather, have exhibited long-term trends. The trends in the relative prices of tradable goods may reflect three different phenomena. First, the composition of tradable goods across countries tends to change over time. As economies develop, their production activities generally shift toward more sophisticated technologies and higher-quality products. Thus, to the extent that price indices for tradable goods are constructed from unit-value data or are not fully adjusted for quality changes, the influence of economic development on the composition of tradable goods is likely to be reflected in gradual trends in the relative prices of tradables across countries. Second, trends in the relative prices of tradables across countries may also reflect trends in the terms of trade among different categories of tradable goods interacting with cross-country differences in price-index weights. Third, changes may have occurred over time in the costs of "goods arbitrage," reflecting the liberalization of trade and foreign exchange restrictions, reductions in transportation costs, or changes in other components of the costs of market penetration.[4] In this regard, the liberalization of trade and payments restrictions has been an important phenomenon for several APEC members during recent decades.

Empirical analysis suggests that policy-related questions about long-run equilibrium exchange rates do not have simple answers. To begin with, the evidence of trends in the relative prices of tradable goods across countries—presumably related in large

[3]For Hong Kong and Taiwan Province of China, data on the relative prices of nontradables were not available.

[4]The trends associated with the first two possible explanations could be quantified, and distinguished from changes associated with the third possibility, if highly disaggregated data were available.

part to permanent changes in the composition of tradable goods or persistent changes in the terms of trade between different tradable goods—suggests that the notion of a long-run equilibrium exchange rate cannot reasonably be defined in terms of a constant purchasing-power-parity (PPP) level for tradable goods. Second, even if aggregate price indices for tradable goods behaved in a manner broadly consistent with long-run PPP, the notion that equilibrium real exchange rates are related to per capita GDP levels in a stable manner would be undermined by evidence of the widely different patterns of change that rapidly growing APEC members have experienced in the relative domestic prices of their nontradable goods.

Questions about appropriate exchange rates in the short-to-medium run, which are also difficult to answer, are not addressed in this study. It is worth emphasizing, however, that—despite the wide range of real exchange rate experiences among the rapidly growing APEC members over the past two decades—it is generally true that rapidly growing economies may often encounter circumstances in which, over a short- to medium-run horizon, policies of allowing greater upward flexibility in nominal and real exchange rates are conducive to preserving or achieving the macroeconomic objectives of internal and external balance.

In addition, in its analysis of the long-run behavior of real exchange rates, Section II abstracts from the possible influences of government policies on the relative domestic price of nontradables and the relative price of tradables across countries. It is clear that such relative prices are affected by changes in the composition of government demand and other fiscal policies, changes in the stances of monetary and exchange rate policies, and various external and internal liberalization measures.

International Trade and Real Exchange Rates

The rapid growth of a number of APEC economies has been widely associated with export expansion and a shift of factors of production into the tradable goods sector. The real exchange rate is a key relative price associated with these structural changes. Section III focuses on the effects of both day-to-day exchange rate volatility and more persistent movements in the real exchange rate on foreign trade flows in the APEC region.

Over the past twenty years, the volume of trade of APEC members as a whole has grown at least one and one-half times as much as the volume of trade in the world in general. This growth was particularly rapid in many of the East Asian economies, while most of the slower rates of growth have been experienced in the more mature economies, paralleling the behavior of real output growth. The type of goods traded also varies significantly among APEC members (see Figure 3-1). Several economies have trade that is heavily concentrated in primary goods (Australia, Chile, New Zealand, and Papua New Guinea). By contrast, the exports of China, Hong Kong, Japan, Korea, Taiwan Province of China, and the United States are highly specialized in manufactured goods. A number of economies, including much of East Asia, fall into an intermediate category, in which exports were predominantly primary goods in the early 1970s but have become more heavily concentrated in manufactured goods over time.

The openness of the various economies in the region to trade (measured as the ratio of the average of nominal merchandise exports and imports to domestic output) also varies widely among APEC members (see Figure 3-3). The two most open economies are Hong Kong and Singapore, which are centers of re-exporting to other markets, as is clearly indicated by the fact that average levels of trade often exceed domestic output. At the opposite end of the scale, the shares of trade in output are lowest for Japan and the United States, the two largest economies in the region. In some other economies the ratios increase rapidly over a limited period, possibly reflecting the impact of trade liberalization; a striking example of this phenomenon is the expansion of trade in China in the 1980s.

There are also important trends within the region regarding intraregional trade. In 1993 approximately two-thirds of all merchandise trade from the APEC region (excluding China, Papua New Guinea, and Brunei Darussalam, where appropriate historical data were not available) went to other economies in this area, up from just over half in 1974. The increase in intra-APEC trade largely reflects the rapid economic expansion of many of the Asian members. The proportion of regional merchandise exports coming from East Asia increased from around 20 percent in 1974 to over 30 percent in 1993. With the important exception of Japan, the East Asian countries have also generally increased the proportions of their imports that they receive from APEC. The most striking feature of these data, however, is the increase in APEC exports going to the United States during the mid-1980s, as the dollar appreciated, and the subsequent reversal of this increase (see Figure 3-4). The appreciation of the U.S. dollar clearly had a significant, if temporary, impact on regional trade patterns.

Bilateral trade patterns also show some interesting features, largely revolving around the United States and Japan (see Figure 3-5). Japan's export share is significantly larger than Japan's import share in trade with both the United States and the newly industrializing Asian economies (NIEs)—Hong Kong, Korea, Singapore, and Taiwan Province of China—a pattern that is repeated for the NIEs in trade with the United States. Hence, the NIEs generally have a triangular trading relationship, being net importers from Japan and net exporters to the United States. A similar, although less strong, pattern is true of other Asian economies as a bloc.[5] By contrast, the South Pacific economies[6] have the opposite triangular arrangement, being net importers from the United States and net exporters to Japan. Finally, the other American economies[7] have trade that is dominated by bilateral ties with the United States.

The triangular trading relationship of the NIEs, other Asian, and Pacific economies makes their economies particularly susceptible to changes in the yen-dollar exchange rate. For example, an appreciation of the yen against the dollar (compared with trend) tends to generate a rise in the prices of imports compared with prices of exports for those countries that are net importers from Japan and net exporters to the United States (a depreciation of the yen against the dollar has the opposite effect). The effects of these movements in the terms of trade, however, could be mitigated by these countries' competition against Japanese goods in the U.S. market. In any case, changes in the yen-dollar exchange rate can have important economic implications for other countries in the region.

The level of the exchange rate has played a central role in empirical work on trade, where volumes of exports and imports are usually related to changes in relative prices and to changes in real activity either at home (for imports) or abroad (for exports). Such equations have proven to be highly successful empirically, and they have consistently been used in policy work and macroeconomic models. Some new empirical estimates of real exchange rate elasticities for the APEC economies are reported in Section III. They indicate that the standard empirical model of trade appears to work fairly well for the APEC region, a conclusion that is supported by similar work on the region by others. More specifically, the results indicate that, for the average APEC economy, a sustained 1 percent depreciation in the real exchange rate reduces import volumes by about ½ of 1 percent and raises real exports by about ¾ of 1 percent. These responses are sufficiently large to ensure that the nominal trade balance improves. The improvement in the trade balance, however, may become apparent only after a year or two. This is because the

impact of a change in the real exchange rate on trade volumes increases significantly over time, which is a standard empirical result.

Given the large differences in openness and the importance of trilateral trading relationships in the APEC region, it is of interest to consider the likely effects on trade of changes in the real exchange rate between the dollar and the yen, the two key currencies in the region. Highly stylized estimates of the impact of bilateral changes between the U.S. dollar and the yen on the one hand and other regional currencies on the other indicate that the economies of the region can be divided into three categories. Canada and Mexico are relatively sensitive to changes in the real value of the U.S. dollar while being fairly insulated from movements in the yen. The extremely open economies of Hong Kong and Singapore are highly sensitive to changes in the real values of both the U.S. dollar and the yen, as is Malaysia. Finally, the vast majority of economies in the region are also dependent on both exchange rates, but to a rather lesser extent than Hong Kong, Malaysia, and Singapore.

Apart from analyzing the effects of sustained changes in the value of the exchange rate, a number of studies have looked at the connection between the day-to-day volatility of the exchange rate and the level of trade. The results from these studies have varied quite widely—with a few finding significant effects from volatility, but with most finding little or no impact. The latter result is particularly true in some of the more recent work using larger data sets. Overall, the evidence appears to point to a small direct effect of exchange rate volatility on trade volumes.

This observation appears at odds with concerns often expressed by business people about floating exchange rates. One explanation may be that higher short-term volatility has been associated with larger, and more persistent, exchange rate misalignments. Such misalignments clearly involve substantial economic costs; for example, an appreciation of a currency can produce significant dislocation for both exporters and import-competing sectors and can increase protectionist pressures. Another explanation could be that in many cases floating exchange rates may have been associated with more unstable macroeconomic policies. Such indirect influences, which are unlikely to be captured in econometric studies that relate exchange rate volatility to trade volumes, may also help to explain the dichotomy between the empirical evidence and the widespread concerns about exchange rate volatility among policymakers.

To summarize the main policy conclusions of Section III, day-to-day volatility of exchange rates does not appear to be a major direct impediment to trade

---

[5]Indonesia, Malaysia, the Philippines, and Thailand.
[6]Australia and New Zealand.
[7]Canada, Chile, and Mexico.

in the APEC region. More sustained movements in exchange rates from year to year, however, do have a significant impact on trade volumes and on the nominal trade balance, although in the latter case the effect may only become apparent after a year or two. Given the joint importance of the United States and Japan in the trade patterns of most other countries in the region, movements in either of the major regional currencies can have a significant impact on trade and activity of the other APEC economies. Finally, the trilateral trading pattern of many of the APEC economies further complicates this situation, as movements in the bilateral rate of the U.S. dollar against the yen also create changes in the relative prices of exports and imports. Changes in the yen-dollar exchange rate can therefore have important implications for the economic welfare of other countries in the region.

Foreign Direct Investment and the Exchange Rate

FDI has become an important source of fixed investment in developing countries and technological transfers from industrial to developing countries. Unlike portfolio investment, which may be withdrawn quickly, FDI is thought to involve a long-term commitment from investors and to be unambiguously beneficial to host countries, contributing to higher rates of long-run growth.

Section IV focuses on FDI and its sensitivity to the exchange rate in the APEC economies. FDI represents the foreign acquisition of a controlling claim on domestic enterprises or land, or further investment in an enterprise that is controlled.[8] It is the word "controlling" that distinguishes FDI from foreign portfolio investment, the other subcategory of private foreign investment.[9] World FDI has grown more rapidly than that of world output or world trade during the past two decades, making it an increasingly important economic link among countries. Several of the APEC economies have been among the fastest-growing hosts of worldwide FDI.

The APEC economies have had varied experiences with inflows and outflows of FDI (see Figure 4-1). In many of the developing economies there has been a clear underlying increase in inward flows of FDI over time, reflecting factors such as high potential returns caused by long-term shifts in productivity, policies of capital account liberalization, and long-term movements in real exchange rates. By

contrast, industrial countries such as Canada, Australia, and New Zealand show no clear trend, presumably reflecting their long tradition of foreign ownership and open capital accounts associated with exploitation of their natural resources. The evidence also shows that there has been significant year-to-year variability of FDI inflows around their underlying trends. Inflows to the United States, for example, rose significantly in the mid-to-late 1980s but fell in the early 1990s. FDI outflows show a similar level of variability. A detailed look at FDI outflows from the United States and Japan, the two most important providers of FDI to the APEC region, further reinforces this conclusion.

These patterns point to the need to explore the role of cyclical factors, such as changes in the exchange rate, as determinants of FDI. Before doing so, however, it is useful to consider the underlying determinants of FDI more generally. The main task involved is explaining why investors need to acquire a controlling interest in a foreign country, rather than simply holding a passive claim—a portfolio share—on that country's output or supplying the market through international trade. One explanation is that multinational firms find it cheaper to expand directly in a foreign country because many of their cost and product advantages rely on internal, indivisible assets such as organizational and technological know-how. Government policies are another major explanation for FDI. Tariffs, quotas, taxes, and subsidies can all create conditions under which it is more (or less) profitable to produce in—rather than export to—a foreign country, a motivation for FDI that is often labeled "tariff-jumping." Empirical evidence supporting these factors as determinants of FDI is ample. The relationship between FDI and trade has also received some attention. Sometimes FDI is seen as a substitute for exports, with local assembly replacing foreign-produced goods, while in other cases FDI is viewed as a complement to exports through its role in building local distribution networks and other facilities in host economies. However, none of these theories is particularly helpful in explaining the behavior of FDI over shorter horizons or across countries that exhibit similar characteristics. Exchange rates, as main determinants of the relative price of domestic and foreign goods and production factors, are prime candidates for this task.

Among the suggested links between the real exchange rate and FDI, the effect of exchange rate changes on domestic costs and asset prices has received the greatest attention. An exchange rate depreciation lowers the cost of domestic production and assets, making investment in the domestic economy more attractive to foreign investors. In addition, a depreciation of the real exchange rate also increases the relative wealth of foreign firms, making

---

[8]Conventionally, investment of 10 percent or more in one company is regarded as a "controlling" claim.

[9]Flows of portfolio investment within APEC are considered in Khan and Reinhart, eds., *Capital Flows in the APEC Region.*

it easier for foreign firms to use cheaper internal financing to buy domestic assets. When considering the effect of exchange rate changes on FDI coming through government policy, an opposite relationship with regard to the real exchange rate can emerge. To the extent that exchange rate depreciations improve a country's trade balance, they may soften protectionist policies and, with it, reduce the incentive for tariff jumping. Further ambiguities arise when going beyond the examination of the effects on FDI of exogenous shocks that cause exchange rates to fall below their long-run trend. Indeed, exchange rates are themselves endogenous variables that respond to a variety of shocks.

Despite these sources of potential ambiguity, several studies (largely on industrial countries) have provided empirical evidence that exchange rate depreciations boost FDI inflows. New empirical work presented in Section IV, which focuses specifically on the APEC region, supports this hypothesis. More specifically, the results indicate that in the average APEC economy a 10 percent appreciation in the real effective exchange rate lowers inflows of FDI by almost ¼ of 1 percent of GDP, a significant proportion of the underlying inflows into most economies. Results are also reported that differentiate flows of FDI from the United States and from Japan to other members of APEC. They provide some preliminary evidence that FDI flows from these two economies may behave somewhat differently with respect to the real exchange rate, with investment from the United States being less dependent on changes in the real exchange rate than the corresponding flows from Japan. This suggests that the factors behind U.S. and Japanese FDI to the rest of the APEC region could be rather different, although more research would be required to sustain such a conclusion.

Attention has also been devoted in the current empirical literature to the effects of greater exchange rate volatility on FDI. Empirical evidence on the link between exchange rate volatility and FDI is limited, but it tends to favor a positive link between exchange rate volatility and FDI inflows. In response to greater exchange rate risk, multinationals appear to increase foreign investment in a country and to reduce exports somewhat.

FDI has increased rapidly over the recent past, and it now represents an important international linkage between members of APEC. Most of the factors affecting underlying levels of FDI flows are strategic, as befits an activity that is long term in nature. This does not mean, however, that short-term factors such as exchange rate fluctuations have no role. As in the case of international trade, there is considerable evidence that changes in the real exchange rate significantly influence movements of FDI compared with trend, with depreciations being associated with increased inflows. Real exchange rate variability may well also increase FDI, although the empirical relationship is less firmly established.

Concluding Perspectives

This Occasional Paper sheds new light on the connection between the dynamism of the APEC economies (in terms of growth in output, trade, and investment) and the behavior of exchange rates. The direction of causality between the exchange rate and economic performance, however, is notoriously difficult to identify; accordingly, care should be taken in using the findings presented here to make policy recommendations. Nevertheless, some general conclusions emerge.

First, countries that have experienced long-term trend appreciations without balance of payments problems have been successful economically, implying that such appreciations are one possible sign of economic success. The converse, however, does not generally hold. In particular, the assumption that high economic growth is associated with long-term real exchange rate appreciations, as high productivity growth in the traded goods sector causes a rise in the price of nontraded goods in comparison with that of traded ones, is found not to be generally true for the APEC region.

Second, for economies facing long-term exchange rate appreciations, it appears unwise to resist the associated nominal exchange rate pressures because the real appreciation will then simply come through higher domestic inflation, with potentially detrimental effects on trade, investment, and growth.

Third, the level of the exchange rate is clearly important for trade and FDI. To the extent that macroeconomic policies and the choice of nominal exchange regime influence the real exchange rate, such policies should ensure that the exchange rate is not allowed to become misaligned.

The diverse levels in economic development among the APEC economies provide a useful sample for looking at the macroeconomic role of exchange rates. Beyond the parameters of the present study, there are various issues that could be examined further, such as identifying the structural characteristics associated with long-term real exchange rate trends and the extent to which the behavior of FDI differs among economies, in particular between the United States and Japan. These tasks are left for future research.

II Long-Run Movements in Real Exchange Rates

Peter Isard and Steven Symansky

Economists have shown little ability to explain exchange rate movements from day to day, month to month, or even year to year. As revealed by several extensive studies undertaken in the early 1980s, which focused on the currencies of major industrial countries, the most widely used structural models of exchange rates could not outperform a naive random-walk model over horizons of twelve months or less, even in predicting the realized behavior of exchange rates using the realized values of the "exogenous" explanatory variables (Meese and Rogoff, 1983a and 1983b). Moreover, subsequent efforts to improve the structural models have achieved very limited success in outperforming the random-walk model over short-term horizons.[1]

Much greater success has been achieved, however, in explaining the behavior of exchange rates over relatively long time intervals. More specifically, nominal exchange rates and ratios of national price or cost levels have been observed to change by similar orders of magnitude over long periods. This can be seen in Figure 2-1, for example, which plots for each APEC member the average annual percentage change in its nominal exchange rate against the U.S. dollar over the period 1973–94 (vertical axis) versus the average annual percentage change in the ratio of its GDP deflator to the U.S. GDP deflator (horizontal axis). The chart shows a strong correlation between changes in nominal exchange rates and changes in ratios of national price levels over the past two decades. Although the average annual changes have been approximately the same in many cases,[2] in some instances they have differed considerably. Consistently, a growing literature has challenged the appropriateness of models that assume that nominal exchange rates and ratios of national price levels have identical trends over the long run.[3]

Models of the long-run behavior of exchange rates are particularly relevant for assessing the extent to which observed changes in currency values are likely to persist. Accordingly, economists are continuing to address a number of unresolved issues about the nature of the long-run relationships between exchange rates and national price or cost levels. This section reviews these issues and summarizes existing attempts to shed light on them empirically. It also examines empirical evidence from the APEC region,[4] which presents a wide range of economic experiences, including a number of economies in which real output has expanded rapidly, thus providing an attractive focus for a study of the long-run behavior of exchange rates.

Historical Perspectives for the APEC Region

The theories addressed in this section focus on the behavior of nominal exchange rates relative to various ratios of national price or cost levels. The ratio of the domestic national price level (P) to the foreign price level (P^*), after multiplying by the nominal exchange rate (S) to convert domestic prices into foreign currency units, is commonly referred to as the real exchange rate (Q):

$$Q = SP/P^*. \qquad (2\text{-}1)$$

Widely used measures of real exchange rates include those based on ratios of GDP deflators, consumer price indices, wholesale price indices, export price indices, and unit labor costs.[5]

Figure 2-2 shows time series of annual data on four different real exchange rate measures for each of

---

[1]See the recent surveys by Frankel and Rose (forthcoming), Isard (1995), and Taylor (1995a, 1995b).

[2]Figure 2-1 includes a 45-degree line for comparison.

[3]See Boucher Breuer (1994), Froot and Rogoff (forthcoming), and Rogoff (1996) for reviews of the relevant literature.

[4]The extent to which the relevant theories can be tested empirically depends on whether the available data on employment and capital stocks are adequate for constructing quantitative measures of labor productivity or total factor productivity in the tradables and nontradables sectors. For most APEC members such data are inadequate. Nevertheless, other data available for APEC members are sufficient to illustrate a number of relevant points about the long-run behavior of exchange rates.

[5]See Clark and others (1994), Marsh and Tokarick (1994), and Turner and Van't dack (1993) for recent theoretical and empirical assessments of how well the different measures of real exchange rates capture international price and cost competitiveness.

Figure 2-1. Nominal Exchange Rates and Ratios of GDP Deflators[1]
(Average annual percent change, 1973–94)

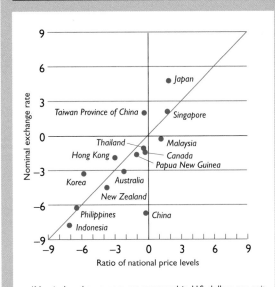

[1]Nominal exchange rates are measured in U.S. dollars per unit of local currency. The ratio of price levels is the U.S. GDP deflator divided by the domestic GDP deflator. Annual averages are based on the data available within the 1973–94 period. For Chile and Mexico, not shown, the horizontal and vertical coordinates are (–21.3, –21.7) and (–24.6, –23.8), respectively.

the APEC members vis-à-vis the United States.[6] Three of the real exchange rate measures—in particular, those based on GDP deflators, consumer price indices, and export price indices—are constructed as the nominal exchange rate (in U.S. dollars per unit of domestic currency) multiplied by the relevant domestic price level divided by the corresponding U.S. price level.[7] By contrast, the real exchange rates based on Penn price relatives are constructed from estimates of the relative domestic and U.S. prices for individual product categories, without using data on nominal exchange rates (a detailed description is provided in the discussion of empirical evidence, below).[8] The graphs in Figure 2-2 start in 1960 but in some cases are limited by data availability. Figure 2-3

shows corresponding time series of multilateral real exchange rates based on national-source GDP deflators, along with the associated bilateral rates vis-à-vis both Japan and the United States.

Figure 2-2 reveals that, for most APEC members, the different measures of real exchange rates have diverged significantly over certain periods while also exhibiting fairly similar cyclical behavior.[9] The discussion of the empirical evidence and the conclusions suggested by the analysis (below) focus on the relevance of both the cyclical similarities and the differences in long-run trends. Figure 2-3 shows that in virtually all cases the overall changes in multilateral rates have been somewhere in between the overall changes in bilateral rates against the dollar and against the yen; this reflects the importance to APEC members of trade with both Japan and the United States, together with the overall appreciation of the yen against the dollar. Figures 2-2 and 2-3 also reveal striking contrasts in exchange rate trends among different APEC members. With regard to the real exchange rates based on GDP deflators, consumer price indices, and Penn price relatives, Japan, Korea, and Taiwan Province of China have experienced substantial real appreciations vis-à-vis the United States since 1973; several other APEC members have experienced small-to-moderate depreciations; and China and Indonesia have had substantial depreciations.

In analyses of long-run trends in real exchange rates among the industrial countries, the real appreciation of the yen over the past two decades is generally associated with the relatively rapid expansion of output in Japan. As the analysis in this section shows, however, data for the APEC region suggest that the long-run relationship between output growth and real exchange rate appreciation is not robust. In particular, there are several members of APEC in which output growth since 1973 has been significantly more rapid than in Japan, while real exchange rates (vis-à-vis the United States) have not appreciated. Some reasons why rapid output growth has not always been accompanied by real exchange rate appreciation are ad-

---

[6]There is no chart for the United States because all variables are measured relative to the U.S. dollar, or for Brunei Darussalam, whose currency notes are exchangeable at par with those of Singapore.

[7]The time series on these three measures, based on data from national sources, are from the IMF's International Financial Statistics and World Economic Outlook databases.

[8]Data on the Penn measures, in which price relatives (domestic versus United States) for individual products are aggregated with weights that reflect shares in domestic real GDP, are from the Penn World Table; see Summers and Heston (1991).

[9]Some of the divergence between the different real exchange rate measures might be attributable to problems of data quality. Accordingly, as a crude way of identifying data series that might be suspect, we looked for contrasts among four real exchange rate measures: the real exchange rate based on GDP deflators, the Penn measure constructed with GDP weights, the real exchange rate based on consumer price indices, and an alternative Penn measure constructed with weights that reflect consumption shares. Except in the cases of Indonesia and Korea, the four measures appear to be reasonably consistent. For Indonesia, the real exchange rate based on national-source GDP deflators is a clear outlier, while for Korea the measure based on national-source consumer price indices is the outlier.

Figure 2-2. Real Exchange Rates vis-à-vis the United States
(1973 = 100)

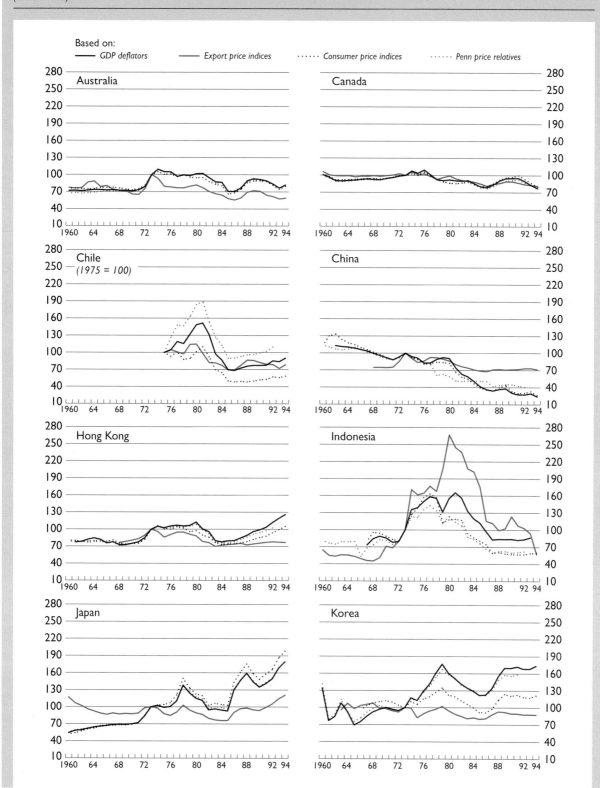

Figure 2-2 *(concluded)*

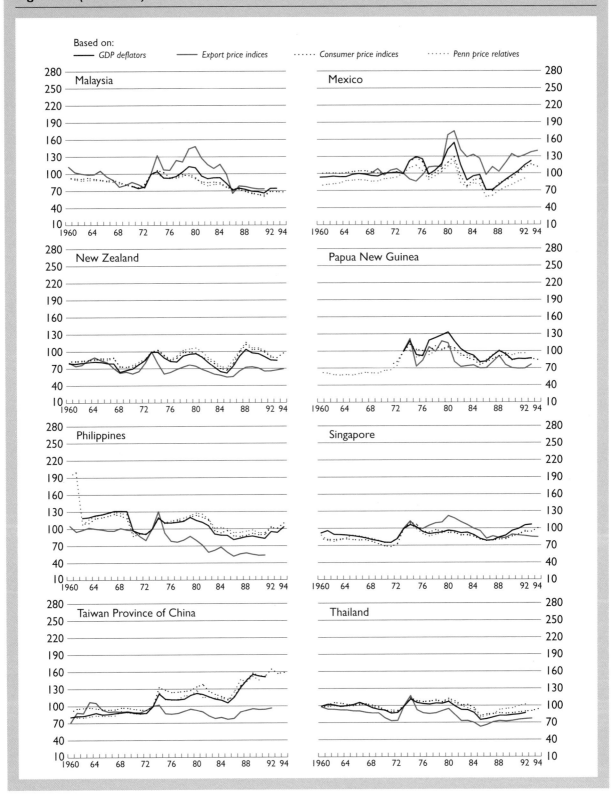

Figure 2-3. Multilateral and Bilateral Real Exchange Rates[1]
(1973 = 100)

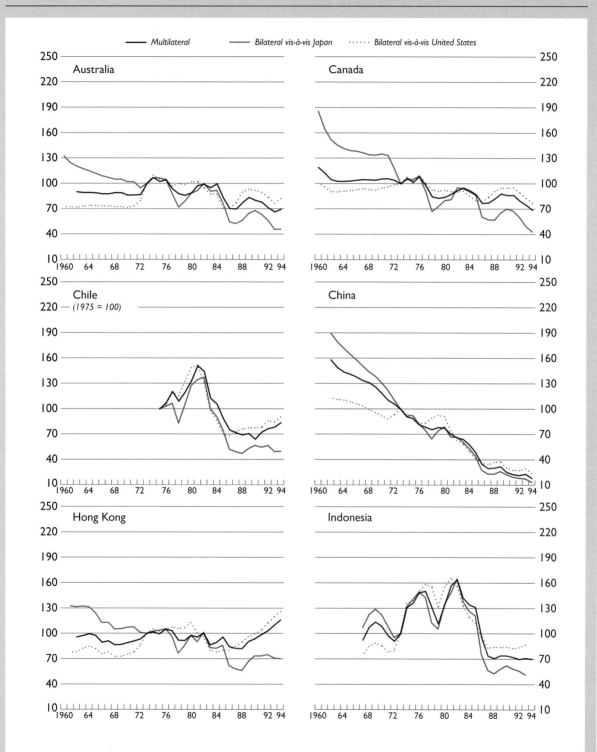

Figure 2-3 *(continued)*

Figure 2-3 *(concluded)*

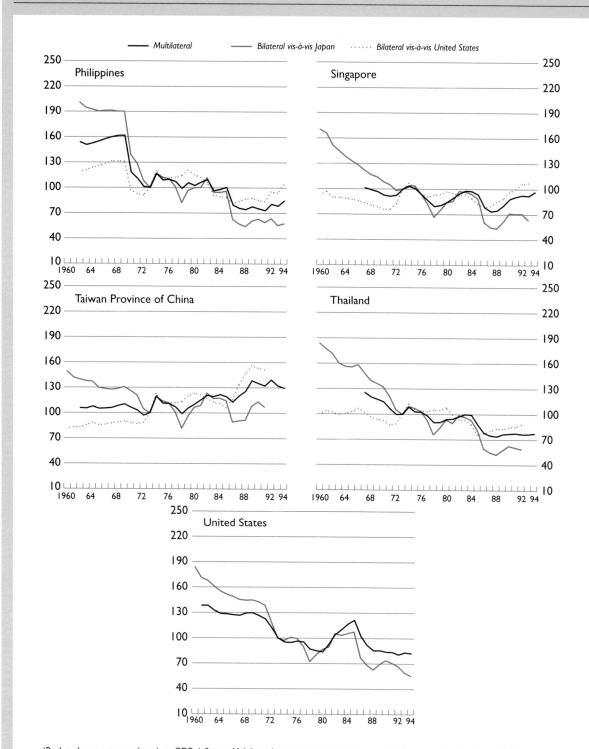

¹Real exchange rates are based on GDP deflators. Multilateral rates are constructed using IMF Information Notice System (INS) total competitiveness weights, in which the weight of country *c* in the multilateral exchange rate for country *j* reflects the degree to which goods produced by the two countries compete directly in the home markets of countries *c* and *j* and indirectly in third markets (see McGuirk, 1987).

dressed in the discussion of the empirical evidence, below.

Table 2-1 provides perspectives on the history of payments restrictions among APEC members, which may have some bearing on the range of exchange rate experiences. In particular, the table lists the time periods since the end of 1973 during which the members of APEC maintained restrictions on payments for current and capital transactions. For example, China restricted payments for both current and capital transactions during the entire period from the end of 1973 through the end of 1993. Thus, nominal exchange rates for the yuan during that period did not reflect market forces to the same extent as nominal exchange rates for the yen, which may partly explain why China is a significant outlier in Figure 2-1. Accordingly, theories about the behavior of real exchange rates in Japan (or other countries without extensive payments restrictions) cannot be applied to, or rejected by, the behavior of real exchange rates in China (or other countries with extensive payments restrictions). More generally, in analyzing the behavior of real exchange rates for APEC economies during the period since the end of 1973, it may be important to bear in mind that six APEC members (Chile, China, Korea, Mexico, Philippines, and Taiwan Province of China) maintained restrictions on payments for both current and capital transactions during substantial parts of the period.

Theories of the Long-Run Behavior of Exchange Rates

Theories of the relationship between nominal exchange rates and ratios of national price or cost levels have been traced back to the sixteenth century and have been linked to the development of the quantity theory of money.[10] Spanish economists were particularly influential in the development of these theories, which presumably were catalyzed by the large increases in money supplies and prices that Spain experienced in association with substantial inflows of gold and silver from newly discovered America. Today, the theory that nominal exchange rates move in parallel with ratios of national price or cost levels is commonly referred to as the hypothesis of "purchasing power parity," a term coined by Gustav Cassel (1918, 1922). Cassel's prolific writings on the purchasing-power-parity (PPP) hypothesis were stimulated by the general inflation that accompanied World War I.

Table 2-1. Payments Restrictions Maintained by APEC Members, 1974–93

| Member | Dates of Payments Restrictions on | |
	Current transactions	Capital transactions
Australia	None	1974–84
Canada	None	None
Chile	1974–76, 1982–93	Entire period
China	Entire period	Entire period
Hong Kong	None	None
Indonesia	1977	None
Japan	None	1974–79
Korea	1974–78, 1982–88	Entire period
Malaysia	None	None
Mexico	1982–87	1982–93
New Zealand	None	1974–84
Papua New Guinea	None[1]	Entire period[1]
Philippines	1973–85, 1986–93	Entire period
Singapore	None	1974–8
Taiwan Province of China	1973–79[2]	1973–79[2]
Thailand	None	Entire period
United States	None	None

Source: Summary tables in the IMF's *Annual Report on Exchange Arrangements and Exchange Restrictions* (Washington, various issues).

[1]Refers to period beginning on October 9, 1975, when Papua New Guinea became a member of the IMF.

[2]Not included in summary tables for the period since 1979.

The PPP hypothesis has received considerable attention in the economic literature during the past two decades.[11] PPP has been thoroughly discredited as a hypothesis about the behavior of nominal exchange rates in the short run. However, extensive econometric work has verified that real exchange rates for industrial countries tend to revert toward their historical averages over long periods of time, which suggests that PPP has some degree of validity in the long run.[12]

An important modification or refinement of the long-run PPP hypothesis has come from the observation that prices of nontradable goods and services, relative to prices of tradables, tend to be higher in high-income countries than in low-income countries. This observation emerged from attempts to make

---

[10]See Einzig (1962) and Officer (1982), who both cite Grice-Hutchinson (1952).

[11]See Dornbusch (1992), Isard (1995), and Rogoff (1996) for summary discussions.

[12]See Boucher Breuer (1994) and Froot and Rogoff (forthcoming) for recent surveys of the extensive econometric literature.

quantitative comparisons of living standards in different countries in a series of projects sponsored by the United Nations and other international organizations, and spearheaded to a large extent by economists from the University of Pennsylvania.[13] These studies have established that the methodology of comparing international standards of living by converting national accounts data at market exchange rates into a common currency unit generally understates the living standards of low-income countries relative to those of high-income countries.[14] Samuelson (1994) referred to this empirical regularity as "the Penn effect."

Balassa (1964) and Samuelson (1964) attempted to explain the Penn effect, along with the associated tendency for exchange rates to deviate systematically from PPP over the long run,[15] by conjecturing that the tendency for the relative price of nontradables to be higher in high-income countries reflected a tendency for productivity in the tradable goods sector to rise relative to productivity in the nontradables sector as real incomes expanded. Given competitive pressures within each country for workers with similar skills to receive similar wages in the two sectors, relatively rapid productivity growth in the tradables sector would tend, other things being equal, to push up the relative cost of production in the nontradables sector and, hence, the relative price of nontradables. Under conditions in which the relative price of tradable goods across countries remained constant, such an increase in the relative price of nontradables would in turn give rise (as clarified in the equations below) to an appreciation of the real exchange rate.

Although changes in the relative price of nontradables have received emphasis in models of deviations from long-run PPP, other factors can also affect the behavior of real exchange rates over the long run. To provide a simple framework for analysis, it is useful to write the aggregate price levels for two countries (P and P^*) as arithmetic weighted averages of the prices of nontradables (P_N and P_N^*) and the prices of tradables (P_T and P_T^*):

$$P = nP_N + (1 - n)P_T \qquad (2\text{-}2)$$

$$P^* = n^*P_N^* + (1 - n^*)P_T^*. \qquad (2\text{-}3)$$

The weights (n and n^*) can be regarded as the shares of nontradables in production when P is interpreted as a GDP deflator, or as shares of nontradables in consumption when P represents a consumer price index.

It is useful to denote the relative common-currency price of tradables in the two countries as

$$b = SP_T/P_T^*, \qquad (2\text{-}4)$$

where, under the convention that the variables marked with an asterisk (*) refer to the foreign country, S is the nominal exchange rate measured in foreign currency per unit of domestic currency. (Hence, an increase in S corresponds to a nominal appreciation of the domestic currency.) It is often hypothesized that the relative price of tradables across countries is time invariant and equal to unity, reflecting the assumption that tradable goods have identical common-currency prices in all countries.[16] Here, however, it is instructive to consider the more general case. It is convenient to define

$$F = P/P_T = (1 - n) + n(P_N/P_T) \qquad (2\text{-}5)$$

$$F^* = P^*/P_T^* = (1 - n^*) + n^*(P_N^*/P_T^*). \qquad (2\text{-}6)$$

And it is then straightforward to show that

$$Q = SP/P^* = bF/F^* = b[(1 - n) + n(P_N/P_T)]/ \\ [(1 - n^*) + n^*(P_N^*/P_T^*)]. \qquad (2\text{-}7)$$

Condition (2-7) describes a general relationship between the real exchange rate (Q), the relative prices of nontradables within each of the two countries (P_N/P_T and P_N^*/P_T^*), the weights of nontradables in the domestic and foreign price indices (n and n^*), and the relative price of tradables across countries (b). The equation confirms that, other things being equal, a rise in the domestic relative price of nontradables (P_N/P_T) leads to a real appreciation. More generally, however, it indicates that changes in real exchange rates over the long run can logically be related to different combinations of changes in the relative price of tradables across countries, changes in both domestic and foreign price-index weights, and changes in both the domestic and foreign relative price of nontradables. In turn, changes in relative prices within countries, price-index weights, and perhaps the relative price of tradables across countries may be reflections of changes in deeper fundamentals, such as changes in

---

[13]See, for example, Gilbert and Kravis (1954); Kravis, Heston, and Summers (1982); and Summers and Heston (1991).

[14]The nature of these studies is described in more detail in the discussion of the empirical evidence, below.

[15]Harrod (1939) provided an earlier discussion of some of the key arguments made by Balassa and Samuelson, the seeds of which have been traced back to Ricardo in 1821 (see Ricardo, 1951).

[16]If P_T and P_T^* are index numbers, the assumption of identical common-currency prices would imply a time-invariant value of b, but not necessarily that $b = 1$.

productivity or shifts in the composition of aggregate demand.[17]

As is readily apparent, condition (2-7) provides a framework for describing the behavior of real exchange rates when only two types of goods are distinguished. In some contexts it may be preferable to distinguish among three types of goods—nontradables and two classes of tradables—in order to consider shifts in the terms of trade between exportables and importables, or to analyze supply shocks that are beneficial to an emerging tradable goods sector but harmful to an older tradables sector.

Empirical Methodologies and Findings from Studies of OECD Economies

A number of economists have conducted empirical tests of structural models of deviations from PPP.[18] A major stimulus to the literature came from Balassa (1964, 1973), who regressed a measure of the deviation from PPP on GNP per capita and found a significant positive correlation using data for 1960 from a cross section of 12 industrial countries. As mentioned earlier, Balassa hypothesized that the correlation reflected the effects of output growth on relative productivity levels and the relative price of nontradables.

Subsequent tests have looked for more direct evidence that real exchange rates are correlated with productivity levels or other determinants of the relative price of nontradables, such as the composition of aggregate demand. For the most part, these tests have looked at real exchange rates based on GDP deflators or consumer price indices and have focused on time-series data for member countries of the Organization for Economic Cooperation and Development (OECD).[19] Although some of these tests have

sought to explain changes over time in such measures of the real exchange rate, others have sought to explain changes over time in the relative price of nontradables (P_N/P_T).[20]

The Balassa-Samuelson hypothesis focuses on the effects of supply-side factors (that is, productivity levels) on relative prices and real exchange rates. It ignores the effects of demand-side factors on relative prices, which may be reasonable for purposes of long-run analysis.[21] In particular, demand-side factors will not have long-run effects on relative prices if factors of production are perfectly mobile between the tradables and nontradables sectors over the long run and if there are constant returns to scale in each sector. In the short-and-medium run, however, demand-side factors, such as the composition of government spending, may have significant effects on the relative price of nontradables. Accordingly, several studies based on annual time-series data have investigated the relevance of demand-side factors.[22]

The empirical evidence from studies of OECD economies suggests two general conclusions about the Balassa-Samuelson hypothesis. One finding is that changes in relative productivity levels for the tradables and nontradables sectors are fairly significant in explaining changes in the relative price of nontradables (P_N/P_T) (De Gregorio, Giovannini, and Wolf, 1994; Asea and Mendoza, 1994). A second finding is that, for the specification forms tested by existing studies, neither productivity differentials

---

[17]The direction of causation in condition (2-7) is not simply from the right-hand-side variables (or their deeper determinants) to Q. For example, changes in nominal exchange rates, which affect both Q and b directly, may induce adjustments in tradable goods prices and, hence, in the relative price of nontradables. Thus, the year-to-year behavior of the relative price of nontradables may reflect nominal exchange rate variability, as well as shifts in the composition of demand or longer-run trends in productivity and other supply-side factors. To this extent, economies that have maintained relatively tight capital controls might be expected to have experienced smaller year-to-year fluctuations in the relative prices of their nontradables, other things being equal.

[18]Froot and Rogoff (forthcoming) provide a recent review of the literature.

[19]The first applications of time-series data to test the Balassa-Samuelson hypothesis included Hsieh (1982), Marston (1987), and Edison and Klovland (1987). These tests employed measures of relative labor productivity levels in the tradables and nontradables sectors, constructed from data on value added and employment. The classification of sectors was fairly arbitrary, with differences among the studies. Hsieh (1982) equated the tradable

goods sector with manufacturing and treated GDP other than manufacturing as nontradables. Marston (1987) defined agriculture and manufacturing as tradables and defined construction and all other services except electricity-gas-water as nontradables; mining and electricity-gas-water were excluded from his analysis because of a desire to abstract from products with a high energy content. Edison and Klovland (1987) defined agriculture, mining, manufacturing, construction, and electricity-gas-water as "commodity sectors" (tradables) and all services except construction and electricity-gas-water as "service sectors" (nontradables). In some subsequent studies, measures of labor productivity have been replaced with estimates of total factor productivity; see De Gregorio, Giovannini, and Wolf (1994) and Asea and Mendoza (1994). As another innovation, in some studies the methodology for classifying individual production sectors as tradables or nontradables has been based on whether the share of exports in sectoral value added exceeds some predecided threshold level; this approach was introduced by De Gregorio, Giovannini, and Wolf (1994).

[20]The latter ratio is sometimes also referred to as a real exchange rate in the context of models in which tradables have identical (common-currency) prices across countries.

[21]This does not imply that it is reasonable to ignore the long-run effects of demand-side factors on the other terms that enter condition (2-7), such as the shares of nontradables in production or consumption. This issue is discussed in Froot and Rogoff (1991).

[22]For example, Froot and Rogoff (1991); Rogoff (1992); De Gregorio, Giovannini, and Krueger (1994); and De Gregorio, Giovannini, and Wolf (1994). See also Bergstrand (1991), who found evidence of demand-side effects in cross-section data.

nor relative prices have been highly significant in explaining the behavior of the broader concept of the real exchange rate (Q) (Froot and Rogoff, 1991; Asea and Mendoza, 1994). As will be shown below, these findings can be reconciled with each other by recognizing that the latter studies have been based on specifications embodying an assumption that is not supported by the data—that the relative price of tradable goods across countries is time invariant.

Empirical Evidence for the APEC Region

As a first step in analyzing real exchange rates for the APEC region, it is interesting to focus on the extent to which the Penn effect is evident in cross-section data. For this purpose, Figure 2-4 shows data on real exchange rates constructed from Penn price relatives, paired with per capita GDP levels, for the cross section of APEC members during 1973, 1983, and 1992. As defined and estimated in international comparisons of living standards, the real exchange rates shown in the chart are constructed solely from price and quantity data, without using data on market exchange rates.[23] Specifically, a country's real exchange rate based on Penn price relatives represents the ratio of the cost of its bill of goods at national prices to the cost of the same bill of goods at international prices.[24] The per capita GDP measures (throughout this section) represent national accounts data converted at 1990 exchange rates into constant (1990) U.S. dollars.[25]

---

[23]The data were obtained from the Penn World Table; see Summers and Heston (1991).

[24]See Summers and Heston (1991); Kravis, Heston, and Summers (1982); or Isard (1983). The United Nations International Comparison Program (ICP) has collected price and expenditure data during several benchmark years for selected countries. Each country in the sample provides data for several hundred items, which are grouped into about 150 "detailed" product categories. The ICP has taken considerable care to define products in ways that are reasonably comparable across countries. For each country in the sample, the ICP records the domestic price of each product category relative to the corresponding price in the United States (the numeraire country), and also divides this relative price into the level of domestic expenditure on the product category to calculate a quantity measure valued at the U.S. price. The international price of the product is then calculated as a quantity-weighted average of national prices. Each country not included in the sample is assumed to have relative price and quantity structures corresponding to the average structures for some particular subset of the countries included in the sample, with the correspondences based on considerations of region and per capita GDP. For years between the sampling benchmarks, extrapolation procedures are used to obtain estimated price and quantity data.

[25]Figure 2-4 would not be altered much if Penn (PPP-adjusted) measures of real GDP were plotted instead of national accounts measures. Only China and Papua New Guinea show significant differences between the two measures of real GDP.

Figure 2-4. Real Exchange Rates and Levels of Per Capita GDP[1]

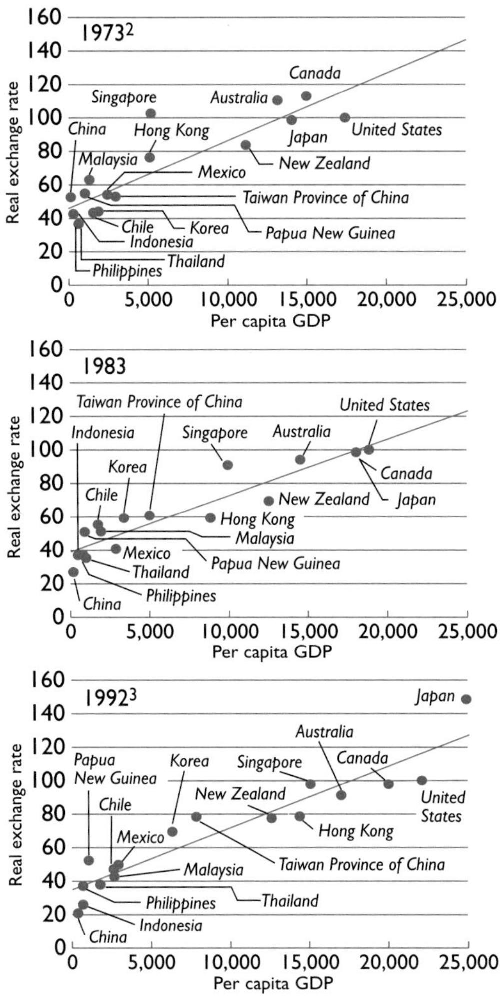

[1]Real exchange rates are based on Penn price relatives.
[2]1975 for Chile.
[3]1990 for Taiwan Province of China; 1991 for Korea.

For each of the three selected years, Figure 2-4 shows a reasonably high positive correlation between real exchange rates and per capita GDP levels. To the extent that it was valid to assume that tradable goods have fairly similar common-currency prices across countries, the correlations shown in the chart would imply that the ratio of nontradables prices to tradables prices was positively correlated with per capita GDP levels.

By contrast with the high cross-section correlations between the *levels* of real exchange rates and

Table 2-2. Real Exchange Rates and Per Capita GDP[1]

APEC Member	1973		1983		1992[2]		Percent Change, 1973–92		Percent Change, 1983–92	
	Real exchange rate	GDP per capita	Real exchange rate	GDP per capita	Real exchange rate	GDP per capita	Real exchange rate	GDP per capita	Real exchange rate	GDP per capita
Australia	110.3	13,187	94.3	14,521	91.1	16,988	−17.4	28.8	−3.4	17.0
Canada	113.1	15,037	99.0	17,998	97.9	19,975	−13.4	32.8	−1.1	11.0
Chile	63.2	1,815	55.5	1,736	47.9	2,652	−24.2	46.1	−13.7	52.8
China	52.4	123	27.0	189	21.3	382	−59.3	209.9	−21.0	101.9
Hong Kong	76.5	5,160	59.3	8,844	78.5	14,370	2.6	178.5	32.4	62.5
Indonesia	42.5	292	37.3	452	26.4	650	−37.8	122.5	−29.1	43.6
Japan	98.5	14,090	98.4	18,026	148.6	24,850	50.8	76.4	50.9	37.9
Korea	44.2	1,857	59.5	3,369	69.9	6,398	58.2	244.6	17.5	89.9
Malaysia	63.1	1,290	51.1	1,939	43.0	2,695	−31.8	109.0	−15.8	39.0
Mexico	54.3	2,399	40.9	2,870	49.2	2,904	−9.4	21.1	20.3	1.2
New Zealand	83.9	11,237	69.6	12,575	77.6	12,640	−7.5	12.5	11.5	0.5
Papua New Guinea	55.1	1,010	50.8	922	52.9	1,025	−3.9	1.4	4.1	11.2
Philippines	36.4	622	37.0	786	37.6	688	3.2	10.6	1.5	−12.5
Singapore	102.3	5,164	90.7	9,927	97.6	15,081	−4.6	192.0	7.5	51.9
Taiwan Province of China	53.5	2,948	60.9	5,020	77.9	7,880	45.5	167.4	27.9	57.0
Thailand	37.2	630	35.5	950	37.9	1,735	2.0	175.4	6.8	82.6
United States	100.0	17,463	100.0	18,877	100.0	22,072	0.0	26.4	0.0	16.9
Correlation coefficient	0.8811		0.9358		0.9421		0.1823		−0.0425	

[1]Real exchange rates are based on Penn price relatives.
[2]1990 for Taiwan Province of China; 1991 for Korea.

per capita GDPs, the correlation between percentage *changes* in real exchange rates and growth rates of GDP per capita have been relatively weak. From Table 2-2, for example, it may be noted that among the eight APEC economies that grew faster than Japan during the 1973–92 period, all but Korea and Taiwan Province of China experienced little if any appreciation of their real exchange rates.[26]

Most empirical attempts to explain the long-run behavior of real exchange rates have looked at conventional measures (for example, real exchange rates based on GDP deflators or consumer price indices) rather than real exchange rates based on the Penn price relatives. Moreover, such studies have focused primarily on time-series data.[27] As

noted earlier, these studies have been relatively successful in explaining the behavior of the ratio of nontradables prices to tradables prices, but not in explaining the behavior of the broader concept of the real exchange rate (Q). In this connection, Figure 2-5 provides scatter plots for APEC members of average annual percentage changes in real exchange rates over the period 1973–92 versus average annual growth rates of GDP per capita. The two different scatter plots reflect two different measures of real exchange rates. The left panel uses bilateral real exchange rates vis-à-vis the United States, based on GDP deflators from national sources. The right panel reflects real exchange rates constructed from the Penn price relatives by using GDP weights. Both plots show weak correlations between the two variables, suggesting that per capita output growth by itself provides a poor explanation of long-run trends in real exchange rates. As in Table 2-2, moreover, Figure 2-5 indicates that among the eight APEC members that exhibited more rapid output growth than Japan during the period 1973–92, only Korea and Taiwan Province of China experienced significant real ap-

---

[26]Similarly, of the nine APEC economies that grew faster than Japan during the 1983–92 period, all but Hong Kong, Korea, and Taiwan Province of China experienced little if any real appreciation.

[27]Cross-section regressions of conventional real exchange rate measures on GDP per capita or other variables make little sense. In particular, since price indices can be normalized to unity in any year, such specifications would be equivalent to regressing the nominal exchange rate on GDP per capita or other variables.

Figure 2-5. Changes in Real Exchange Rates and Per Capital GDP

(Average annual percent change, 1973–92)[1]

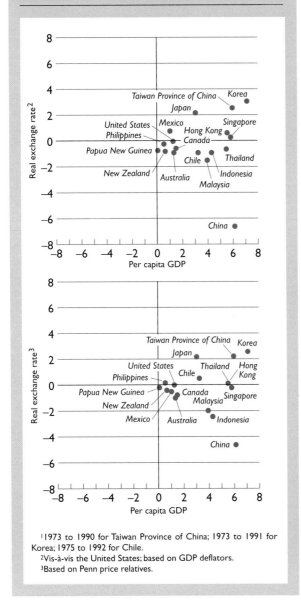

[1]1973 to 1990 for Taiwan Province of China; 1973 to 1991 for Korea; 1975 to 1992 for Chile.
[2]Vis-à-vis the United States; based on GDP deflators.
[3]Based on Penn price relatives.

One place to look for an explanation is in the behavior of productivity growth in the tradables sector relative to productivity growth in nontradables—or, if that is precluded by data limitations, in the behavior of the price of nontradables relative to the price of tradables. Recall that the Balassa-Samuelson conjecture maintains that the ratio of tradables productivity to nontradables productivity is positively correlated with output per capita, and that increases in the productivity ratio push up the price of nontradables relative to the price of tradables, which is positively correlated with the real exchange rate under the assumption that the relative price of tradable goods across countries remains constant.

Young (1995) has recently published relevant estimates of productivity growth for three of the fastest-growing APEC members: Korea, Singapore, and Taiwan Province of China. Young's estimates suggest that, in apparent contradiction of the Balassa-Samuelson hypothesis, for Taiwan Province of China total factor productivity grew significantly faster in services than in manufacturing during 1966–90; while for Singapore, total factor productivity grew significantly faster economy-wide (hence, presumably, in the nontradables sector) than in manufacturing.[29]

For most members of APEC, available data are not adequate for constructing measures of labor productivity or total factor productivity for the tradables and nontradables sectors. Annual data exist, however, on value added broken down into several different categories of output, and on the implicit price deflators associated with each category of output. It is thus possible to test whether productivity growth in tradables has been relatively rapid by examining whether the change in the price of nontradables (services) relative to the price of tradables (manufactures) has been positively correlated with the growth rate of per capita output.[30] Although it is certainly incorrect to assume that manufacturing output is entirely tradable and services entirely nontradable, the ratio of services prices to manufacturing prices

preciations.[28] In contrast, of the eight APEC members with average growth rates below that of Japan, none experienced a significant real appreciation.

Why is it that most of the rapidly growing APEC members did not experience real appreciations?

---

[28]These findings apply as well to a scatter plot based on multilateral real exchange rates.

[29]Young's research focused primarily on explaining the rapid output growth experienced by these three economies and Hong Kong. His findings attribute much of the output growth to the accumulation of factor inputs (physical and human capital, including increases in labor participation rates) rather than to rapid productivity growth.

[30]The price data are taken from the national accounts files of the World Bank's Economic and Social Database. These files contain annual data on nominal value added and real value added (that is, value added at base-year prices) for major sectors of the economy; however, they do not contain the employment data necessary to construct measures of labor productivity by sector. For most APEC members, the available data span the 1973–92 period, at least for the manufacturing and services sectors.

Figure 2-6. Changes in Relative Prices of Nontradables and Per Capita GDP[1]

(Average annual percent change in normalized levels, 1973–92)

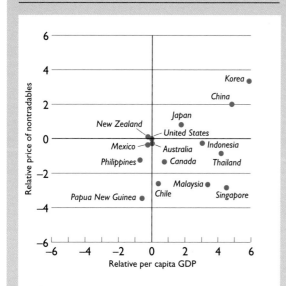

[1]The vertical axis measures the average annual percent change in the ratio of the price of nontradable goods to the price of tradable goods divided by the corresponding ratio for the United States. The horizontal axis measures the average annual percent change in the ratio of domestic per capita GDP to per capita GDP for the United States. Annual averages are based on the data available within the 1973–92 period.

may be a reasonable proxy for the relative price of nontradables.[31]

Figure 2-6 provides a scatter plot of average annual percentage changes in the relative price of nontradables and average rates of growth of output per capita during 1973–92. Korea and China provide examples in which rapid per capita output growth has been associated with a substantial increase in the relative price of nontradables;[32] in contrast, all of the eight APEC members with average growth rates below that of Japan have experienced declines (or very small increases) in the relative prices of their nontradables. Yet it also appears from Figure 2-6 that the Balassa-Samuelson hypothesis is not valid in all cases. In particular, Singapore, Malaysia, Thailand, and Indonesia provide examples of rapidly growing

economies that did not experience increases in the relative prices of nontradables.[33]

A caveat is that such evidence may be distorted to some extent by measurement error in the relative price data, including the distortions that may be introduced in using the ratio of services prices to manufacturing prices as a proxy for the ratio of nontradables prices to tradables prices.[34] In addition, the analysis abstracts from the possibility that the relative price of nontradables may have been affected by changes in government policies—including changes in the composition of demand and changes in the stances of monetary and fiscal policies, as well as external and internal liberalization measures.

Regardless of the role of output (or relative productivity) growth in driving the relative price of nontradables, the real exchange rate is linked to the relative price of nontradables through the system of identities developed above (recall condition (2-7)). In particular, both the long-run trend and the variability over time in the real exchange rate (Q) are reflections of trends or variability in other variables—the relative (common-currency) price of domestic and foreign tradable goods (b), the domestic and foreign relative prices of nontradable goods (P_N/P_T and P_N^*/P_T^*), and the shares of nontradables in the domestic and foreign price indices (n and n^*).

Figure 2-7 shows the relative contributions of these "proximate determinants" in explaining the behavior of real exchange rates over time for individual APEC members. For this purpose the real exchange rate measures have been constructed using condition (2-7), which ensures that the relative contributions of the proximate determinants add up to the total.[35] Table 2-3 provides additional information on the magnitudes of the changes over twenty years (1973 through 1992) in the proximate determinants. The most striking feature of the chart is the behavior of the relative price of tradables across countries. In general, the relative price of tradables across countries has varied widely over time, "explaining" most of the *year-to-year* variation in the real exchange rate. Moreover, in half the cases the *trend* change in the real exchange rate over the twenty-year period can be largely explained by the relative price of tradables across countries. As is evident, however, there

---

[31]In this section, the agricultural sector is not included in either the tradables sector or the nontradables sector. This may bias the analysis when agriculture has a large share in total output and its price moves in a different way from prices for the other sectors.

[32]It may be noted from Figure 2-5, however, that China experienced a substantial depreciation of its real exchange rates.

[33]For Hong Kong and Taiwan Province of China, data on the relative prices of nontradables were not available.

[34]Such distortions may be particularly significant for countries in which much of the services sector consists of business and financial services, which tend to be traded internationally.

[35]The real exchange rates (Q) in Figure 2-7 are analogous to the measures based on GDP deflators in Figure 2-2 and elsewhere in this section; however, the measures in Figure 2-7 are constructed as if GDP consisted only of the output of the manufacturing and services sectors.

Figure 2-7. Real Exchange Rates and Contributions of Proximate Determinants[1]

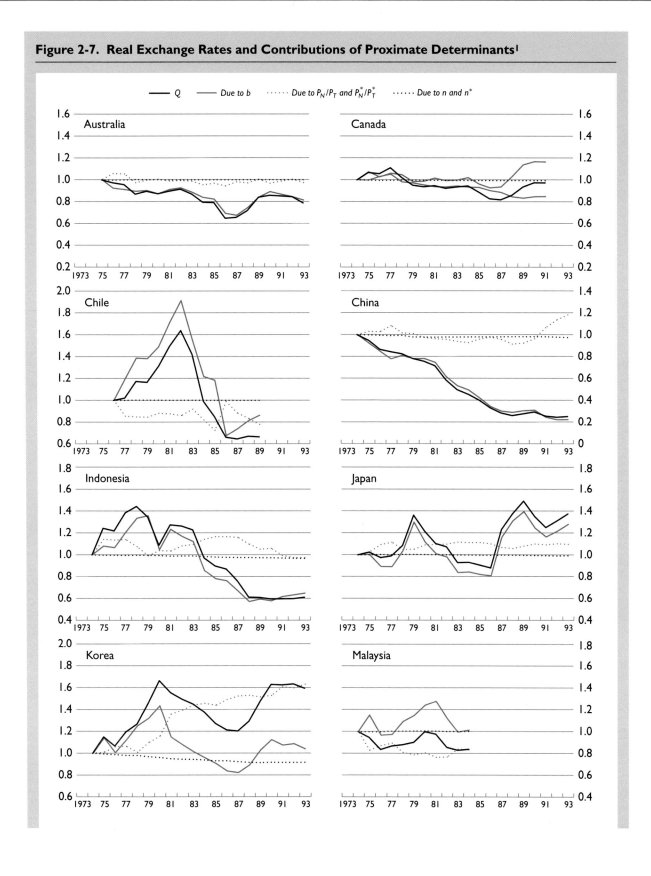

Figure 2-7 *(concluded)*

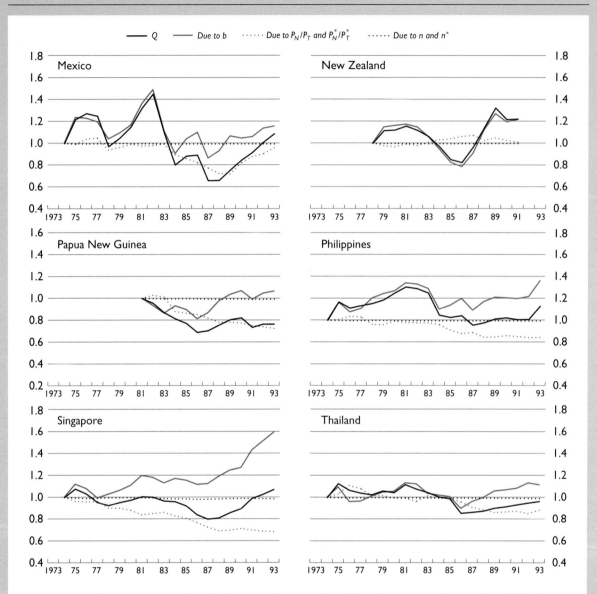

¹The heavy line shows the time path of the real exchange rate relative to the United States (Q) as constructed using condition (2-7) in the text. The line labeled "due to b" (alternatively: P_N/P_T and P_N^*/P_T^*; or n and n^*) shows the path that Q would have taken if only b (alternatively: P_N/P_T and P_N^*/P_T^*; or n and n^*) varied while all other proximate determinants remained constant.

Table 2-3. Real Exchange Rates and Proximate Determinants, 1973 and 1992[1]

	Q			b			n^1			$P_N/P_T{}^1$		
	1973[2]	1992[3]	Percent change	1973[2]	1992[3]	Percent change	1973[2]	1992[3]	Percent change	1973[2]	1992[3]	Percent change
Australia	1.16	0.92	−20.9	1.12	0.91	−18.7	1.03	1.06	2.9	1.06	1.01	−4.8
Canada	1.20	1.19	−0.6	1.07	1.25	16.2	0.89	0.95	7.0	1.19	0.95	−20.4
Chile	1.53	1.03	−32.7	1.36	1.17	−13.8	0.99	0.99	0.1	1.19	0.85	−29.0
China	3.86	0.98	−74.5	4.11	0.91	−77.7	0.80	0.58	−27.6	0.82	1.20	46.0
Indonesia	1.01	0.65	−35.9	1.17	0.76	−35.3	1.13	0.86	−23.8	0.85	0.81	−4.3
Japan	1.14	1.57	36.8	1.24	1.59	27.8	0.88	0.81	−7.7	0.86	1.00	17.0
Korea	0.60	0.97	62.9	0.93	0.97	3.8	1.13	0.82	−27.0	0.55	1.01	86.0
Malaysia	1.13	0.95	−16.4	0.87	0.88	1.1	0.98	0.92	−6.4	1.43	1.10	−23.6
Mexico	0.75	0.83	11.0	0.74	0.85	15.5	1.03	0.95	−7.7	1.04	0.97	−6.3
New Zealand	0.92	1.14	23.3	0.95	1.15	21.6	0.97	0.95	−1.8	0.99	1.01	1.5
Papua New Guinea	1.22	0.95	−22.7	1.08	1.15	6.6	1.07	1.06	−0.7	1.18	0.78	−34.3
Philippines	0.94	1.09	15.8	0.84	1.14	36.0	0.78	0.83	6.2	1.22	0.96	−20.6
Singapore	1.17	1.27	8.6	0.90	1.43	59.4	0.95	0.94	−1.5	1.47	0.85	−41.8
Thailand	1.09	1.07	−1.8	0.95	1.05	11.3	0.98	0.81	−17.9	1.23	1.04	−15.2

[1]Real exchange rates are those shown in Figure 2-7. The proximate determinants n and P_N/P_T are measured as ratios to U.S. levels.

[2]1971 for Canada; 1975 for Chile; 1977 for New Zealand; and 1980 for Papua New Guinea.

[3]1990 for Canada and New Zealand; 1988 for Chile; and 1983 for Malaysia.

are a number of cases—Canada, Korea, Malaysia, Mexico (since 1982), Papua New Guinea, Philippines (since 1982), Singapore, and Thailand (since 1985)—in which changes in real exchange rates have been related significantly to other factors, primarily to changes in the price of nontradables relative to the price of tradables.

Figure 2-8 shows the behavior of real exchange rates based on GDP deflators and two alternative measures of the relative price of tradables across countries—the relative price of manufactures across countries (essentially equivalent to b in Figure 2-7) and the relative price of exports (identical to the real exchange rate based on export prices in Figure 2-2). The latter measure of the relative price of tradables across countries has also exhibited wide year-to-year variability and, in some cases, substantial cumulative change over time. In a number of cases the two alternative measures of the relative price of tradable goods across countries do not move closely in parallel. In most of these cases, the divergence between the relative export price and the relative price of manufactures across countries may reflect a composition of exports that includes large proportions of agricultural products and other nonmanufactured goods. In some cases, however, it may also have been associated with significant divergence between the export prices and domestic prices of manufactured goods, reflecting either a widening or a narrowing trend in profit margins on sales of domestic

manufactures accompanied by the opposite trend in profit margins on export sales.

The year-to-year variability in the relative prices of tradables across countries and the high correlation between these changes and the year-to-year changes in real exchange rates undoubtedly reflect fluctuations in nominal exchange rates (recall the definitions in conditions (2-1) and (2-4)). Moreover, the year-to-year changes in relative prices across countries, as exhibited by aggregate price indices for tradable goods, show deviations from the law of one price for individual tradable goods. One theory of why there can be deviations from the law of one price—in the sense that the same good or similar goods sell for different prices in different markets—is that imperfect competition in the short run enables oligopolistic suppliers to "price to market" and charge different prices for similar products in different countries.[36] A second reason that changes in exchange rates may not be immediately reflected in the relative prices of a good in domestic and foreign markets is that firms may incur various costs when they adjust their prices. A number of economists have attempted to assess the adjustment-cost and pricing-to-market theories of movements in the rela-

---

[36]See Faruqee (1995) and references cited therein. This could explain the upward trend in relative tradable goods prices in Japan in Figure 2-7 compared with the relatively stable behavior of Japanese export prices in Figure 2-2.

Figure 2-8. Real Exchange Rates and Relative Prices Across Countries[1]
(1973 = 100)

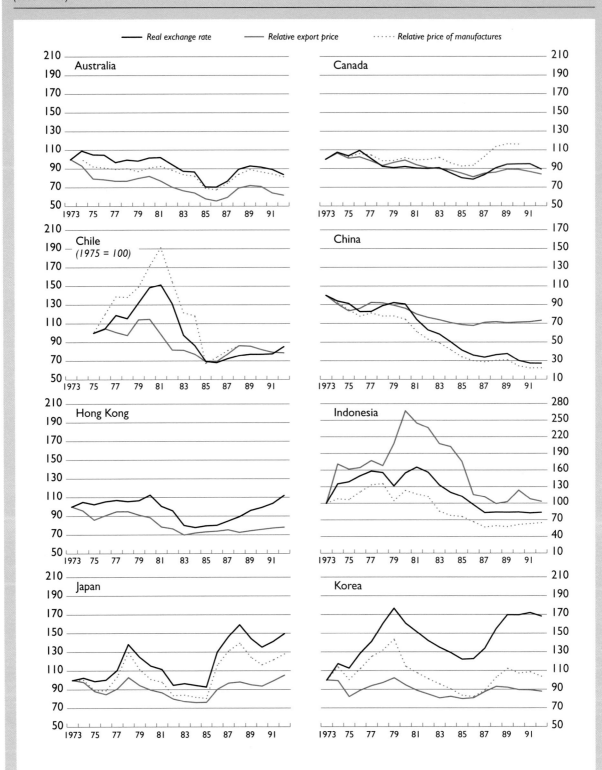

Figure 2-8 *(concluded)*

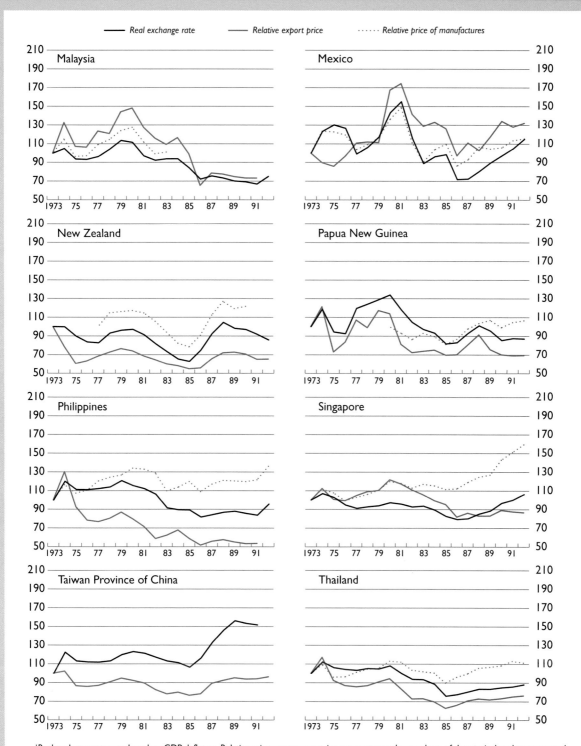

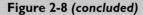

[1]Real exchange rates are based on GDP deflators. Relative prices across countries are constructed as products of the nominal exchange rate and the ratio of the domestic export price index (or price deflator for manufacturing output) to the U.S. export price index (or price deflator for manufacturing output).

tive prices of tradable goods across countries.[37] The two possibilities are not mutually exclusive, and this has made it difficult to determine their relative importance.

In contrast to the year-to-year changes, the substantial cumulative changes over the twenty-year period in the relative prices of tradable goods across countries may be reflections of three different phenomena. One likely part of the explanation is that the composition of tradable goods across countries tends to change over time. As economies develop, their production activities tend to shift toward more sophisticated technologies and higher-quality products.[38] Thus, to the extent that price indices for tradable goods are constructed from unit-value data or are not fully adjusted for quality changes, the influence of economic development on the composition of tradable goods is likely to be reflected in gradual trends in the relative prices of tradables across countries.[39] Another likely part of the explanation is that the observed trends in the relative prices of tradables across countries may reflect trends in the terms of trade among different categories of tradable goods interacting with cross-country differences in price-index weights.

As a third possibility, the explanation may be partly related to changes over time in the costs of "goods arbitrage," reflecting the liberalization of trade restrictions, reductions in transportation costs, or changes in other components of the costs of market penetration. As noted earlier, the liberalization of trade and payments restrictions was an important phenomenon for several APEC members during the 1973–92 period (see Table 2-1).

Concluding Perspectives

Although economists remain mystified by movements in exchange rates from day to day, month to month, and even year to year, there is strong evidence that nominal exchange rates move broadly in parallel with ratios of national price levels over long periods of time. The data also indicate, however, that the parallel is not exact. For some countries—for example, Japan—the trend appreciation in the nominal exchange rate has differed significantly from the trend in the ratio of national price levels.

Whether rapid output growth tends to be associated with real exchange rate appreciation has been a central issue of investigation in conceptual and empirical research on the long-run behavior of exchange rates. The issue has received stimulus from the Balassa-Samuelson conjecture, which states that relatively rapid output growth tends to be associated with more rapid productivity growth in the tradables sector than in the nontradables sector, putting upward pressure on the price of nontradables relative to the price of tradables. To the extent that little change occurs in the relative prices of tradable goods across countries, a rise in the domestic relative price of nontradables is in turn associated with real exchange rate appreciation. This story appears to be widely accepted as a large part of the explanation of the Japanese experience.

Although several fast-growing APEC economies besides Japan have also experienced real exchange rate appreciations over the past two decades, a number of others have not.[40] To help to understand these different experiences, this section developed a definitional identity in which the real exchange rate (as conventionally based on GDP deflators or consumer price indices) is expressed as the product of the ratio of the relative price of domestic and foreign tradable goods, and an expression that increases monotonically with increases in the ratio of the domestic price of nontradables to the domestic price of tradables, other things being equal. The identity suggests that the fact that some rapidly growing APEC economies did not experience real exchange rate appreciations during recent decades may have been related either to changes over time in relative prices of tradables across countries or to decreases in relative domestic prices of nontradables.

This section has examined the empirical evidence on both of these possibilities. To the extent that the data are reliable (and that services and manufactured goods can reasonably be regarded as nontradables and tradables, respectively), they show that Indonesia (since 1985), Malaysia, Singapore, and Thailand all provide counterexamples to the Balassa-Samuelson hypothesis (see Figures 2-6 and 2-7). In these

---

[37]Recent contributions include Froot and Klemperer (1989), Knetter (1989, 1993), Rangan and Lawrence (1993), and Ghosh and Wolf (1994). Froot and Rogoff (forthcoming) provide a brief review of the literature.

[38]Although in this section tradable goods are restricted to manufactured products, the phenomenon of shifting commodity composition is more widespread. Many APEC members, for example, have undergone a significant shift from being primary commodity producers at the beginning of the sample period to being economies with sizable manufacturing sectors in more recent years.

[39]Likewise, to the extent that price indices reflect unit-value data, a significant part of the year-to-year fluctuations in the relative price of tradables across countries may reflect year-to-year changes in the commodity composition of traded goods.

---

[40]Regardless of the correlation between output growth and real appreciation over the long run, any rapidly growing economy may sometimes encounter circumstances in which policies of allowing greater upward flexibility in nominal and real exchange rates are conducive to achieving the macroeconomic objectives of internal and external balance over the medium run.

cases, rapid output growth did not lead to increases in relative domestic prices of nontradables during the 1973–92 period and, therefore, did not lead to real exchange rate appreciation through the Balassa-Samuelson channel.[41] Thus, the data suggest that, in comparisons of these economies with the United States, the "Penn effect"—or the degree to which simple exchange rate conversions distort international comparisons of living standards—would have tended to widen over the two decades had other things been equal.[42] Consistently, despite strong evidence of the Penn effect in cross-section data, time-series data for the 1973–92 period indicate that these fast-growing economies experienced little if any real exchange rate appreciations during the two decades (see Figures 2-4 and 2-5).

The data also reveal that the relative prices of tradable goods across countries have varied considerably from year to year and, for most APEC members, have exhibited substantial trends over time. Thus, even for rapidly growing economies in which productivity growth is higher in the tradable goods sector than in the nontradables sector, the associated pressures on real exchange rates may conceivably be offset by changes in the relative prices of tradable goods across countries. Persistent changes in the latter relative prices may reflect several different phenomena, including changes over time in the composition of tradable goods across countries, changes in the terms of trade among different categories of tradable goods interacting with cross-country differences in price-index weights, or changes over time in the costs of "goods arbitrage" as a result of changes in trade restrictions, transportation costs, or other market penetration costs.

In sum, this section has verified that there is strong evidence of the Penn effect in cross-section data, while also challenging the presumption that fast-growing economies can generally be expected to experience real exchange rate appreciations. In challenging the latter presumption, it was noted, first, that time-series data for some rapidly growing APEC economies appear to provide counter-examples to the Balassa-Samuelson hypothesis and, second, that for aggregate measures of tradable goods prices, there is widespread evidence of trends over several decades in the relative prices of tradable

goods across countries. An interesting issue that the analysis in this section has not addressed is the extent to which the rejections of the Balassa-Samuelson hypothesis can be attributed to the influence of government policies.

References

Asea, Patrick K., and Enrique G. Mendoza, 1994, "The Balassa-Samuelson Model: A General-Equilibrium Appraisal," *Review of International Economics,* Vol. 2 (October), pp. 244–67.

Balassa, Bela, 1964, "The Purchasing-Power-Parity Doctrine: A Reappraisal," *Journal of Political Economy,* Vol. 72 (December), pp. 584–96.

———, 1973, "Just How Misleading Are Official Exchange Rate Conversions? A Comment," *Economic Journal,* Vol. 83 (December), pp. 1258–67.

Bergstrand, Jeffrey H., 1991, "Structural Determinants of Real Exchange Rates and National Price Levels: Some Empirical Evidence," *American Economic Review,* Vol. 81 (March), pp. 325–34.

Boucher Breuer, Janice, 1994, "An Assessment of the Evidence on Purchasing Power Parity," in *Estimating Equilibrium Exchange Rates,* ed. by John Williamson (Washington: Institute for International Economics), pp. 245–77.

Cassel, Gustav, 1918, "Abnormal Deviations in International Exchanges," *Economic Journal,* Vol. 28 (December), pp. 413–15.

———, 1922, *Money and Foreign Exchange After 1914* (New York: Constable).

Clark, Peter B., Leonardo Bartolini, Tamim Bayoumi, and Steven Symansky, 1994, "Exchange Rates and Economic Fundamentals: A Framework for Analysis," Occasional Paper 115 (Washington: International Monetary Fund).

De Gregorio, José, Alberto Giovannini, and Thomas H. Krueger, 1994, "The Behavior of Nontradable-Goods Prices in Europe: Evidence and Interpretation," *Review of International Economics,* Vol. 2 (October), pp. 284–305.

De Gregorio, José, Alberto Giovannini, and Holger C. Wolf, 1994, "International Evidence on Tradables and Nontradables Inflation," *European Economic Review,* Vol. 38 (June), pp. 1225–44.

Dornbusch, Rudiger, 1992, "Purchasing Power Parity," in *The New Palgrave Dictionary of Economics,* Vol. 3, ed. by Peter Newman, Murray Milgate, and John Eatwell (New York: Stockton), pp. 236–44.

Edison, Hali J., and Jan Tore Klovland, 1987, "A Quantitative Reassessment of the Purchasing-Power-Parity Hypothesis: Evidence from Norway and the United Kingdom," *Journal of Applied Econometrics,* Vol. 2 (October), pp. 309–33.

Einzig, Paul, 1962, *The History of Foreign Exchange* (London: Macmillan).

Faruqee, Hamid, 1995, "Pricing to Market and the Real Exchange Rate," *Staff Papers,* International Monetary Fund, Vol. 42 (December), pp. 855–81.

---

[41]Both policy design and inherent comparative advantages may contribute to cases of fast-growing economies in which productivity advances are concentrated in the services sector.

[42]Specifically, in the absence of any changes in the relative price of tradable goods across countries, the quantity of nontradables that could have been obtained in these fast-growing economies in exchange for a given amount of tradables would have increased over time relative to the quantity of nontradables that could have been obtained in exchange for the same amount of tradables in the more slowly growing United States.

Frankel, Jeffrey A., and Andrew K. Rose, forthcoming, "A Survey of Empirical Research on Nominal Exchange Rates," in *Handbook of International Economics,* Vol. 3, ed. by Gene Grossman and Kenneth Rogoff (Amsterdam: North-Holland).

Froot, Kenneth A., and Paul D. Klemperer, 1989, "Exchange-Rate Pass Through When Market Share Matters," *American Economic Review,* Vol. 79 (September), pp. 637–54.

Froot, Kenneth A., and Kenneth Rogoff, 1991, "The EMS, the EMU, and the Transition to a Common Currency," in *1991 NBER Macroeconomics Annual,* ed. by Olivier Blanchard and Stanley Fischer (Cambridge, Mass.: MIT Press), pp. 269–317.

———, forthcoming, "Perspectives on PPP and Long-Run Real Exchange Rates," in *Handbook of International Economics,* Vol. 3, ed. by Gene Grossman and Kenneth Rogoff (Amsterdam: North-Holland).

Ghosh, Atish R., and Holger C. Wolf, 1994, "Pricing in International Markets: Lessons from the Economist," NBER Research Paper 4806 (Cambridge, Mass.: National Bureau of Economic Research, July).

Gilbert, Milton, and Irving B. Kravis, 1954, *An International Comparison of National Products and the Purchasing Power of Currencies: A Study of the United States, the United Kingdom, France, Germany, and Italy* (Paris: Organization for European Economic Cooperation).

Gilbert, Milton, and associates, 1958, *Comparative National Products and Price Levels: A Study of Western Europe and the United States* (Paris: Organization for European Economic Cooperation).

Grice-Hutchinson, Marjorie, 1952, *The School of Salamanca* (Oxford: Clarendon Press).

Harrod, Roy F., 1939, *International Economics,* 5th ed. (1973) (London: Nisbet).

Hsieh, David A., 1982, "The Determination for the Real Exchange Rate: The Productivity Approach," *Journal of International Economics,* Vol. 12 (May), pp. 355–62.

Isard, Peter, 1983, review of Kravis, Heston, and Summers (1982), *Journal of International Economics,* Vol. 15 (August), pp. 177–81.

———, 1995, *Exchange Rate Economics* (Cambridge and New York: Cambridge University Press).

Knetter, Michael, 1989, "Price Discrimination by U.S. and German Exporters," *American Economic Review,* Vol. 79 (March), pp. 198–210.

———, 1993, "International Comparisons of Pricing to Market Behavior," *American Economic Review,* Vol. 83 (June), pp. 473–86.

Kravis, Irving B., Alan Heston, and Robert Summers, 1982, *World Product and Income: International Comparisons of Real Gross Product* (Baltimore: Johns Hopkins University Press).

McGuirk, Anne K., 1987, "Measuring Price Competitiveness for Industrial Country Trade in Manufactures," Working Paper 87/34 (Washington: International Monetary Fund, April).

Marsh, Ian W., and Stephen P. Tokarick, 1994, "Competitiveness Indicators: A Theoretical and Empirical Assessment," IMF Working Paper 94/29 (Washington: International Monetary Fund, March).

Marston, Richard C., 1987, "Real Exchange Rates and Productivity Growth in the United States and Japan," in *Real-Financial Linkages Among Open Economies,* ed. by Sven Arndt and J. David Richardson (Cambridge, Mass.: MIT Press).

Meese, Richard A., and Kenneth Rogoff, 1983a, "Empirical Exchange Rate Models of the Seventies: Do They Fit Out of Sample?" *Journal of International Economics,* Vol. 14 (February), pp. 3–24.

———, 1983b, "The Out-of-Sample Failure of Empirical Exchange Rate Models: Sampling Error or Misspecification?" in *Exchange Rates and International Macroeconomics,* ed. by Jacob A. Frenkel (Chicago: University of Chicago Press), pp. 67–112.

Officer, Lawrence H., 1982, *Purchasing Power Parity and Exchange Rates: Theory, Evidence and Relevance* (Greenwich, Conn.: JAI).

Rangan, Subramanian, and Robert Z. Lawrence, 1993, "The Responses of U.S. Firms to Exchange Rate Fluctuations: Piercing the Corporate Veil," *Brookings Papers on Economic Activity: 2,* pp. 341–69.

Ricardo, David, 1951, *On the Principles of Political Economy and Taxation,* in *The Works and Correspondence of David Ricardo,* Vol. 1, ed. by Piero Sraffa (Cambridge and New York: Cambridge University Press).

Rogoff, Kenneth, 1992, "Traded Goods Consumption Smoothing and the Random Walk Behavior of the Real Exchange Rate," *Bank of Japan Monetary and Economic Studies,* Vol. 10 (November), pp. 1–29.

———, 1996, "The Purchasing Power Parity Puzzle," *Journal of Economic Literature,* Vol. 34 (June), pp. 647–68.

Samuelson, Paul A., 1964, "Theoretical Notes on Trade Problems," *Review of Economics and Statistics,* Vol. 46 (May), pp. 145–54.

———, 1994, "Facets of Balassa-Samuelson Thirty Years Later," *Review of International Economics,* Vol. 2 (October), pp. 201–26.

Summers, Robert, and Alan Heston, 1991, "The Penn World Table (Mark 5): An Expanded Set of International Comparisons, 1950–1988," *Quarterly Journal of Economics,* Vol. 106 (May), pp. 327–68.

Taylor, Mark P., 1995a, "The Economics of Exchange Rates," *Journal of Economic Literature,* Vol. 33 (March), pp. 13–47.

———, 1995b, "Exchange Rate Behavior Under Alternative Exchange Rate Regimes," in *Understanding Interdependence: The Macroeconomics of the Open Economy,* ed. by Peter B. Kenen (Princeton, N.J.: Princeton University Press).

Turner, Philip, and Jozef Van't dack, 1993, "Measuring International Price and Cost Competitiveness," Economic Papers, No. 39 (Basel: Bank for International Settlements).

Young, Alwyn, 1995, "The Tyranny of Numbers: Confronting the Statistical Realities of the East Asian Growth Experience," *Quarterly Journal of Economics,* Vol. 110 (August), pp. 641–80.

III International Trade and Real Exchange Rates

Tamim Bayoumi

The real exchange rate is one of the key relative prices in an economy, defining the rate of exchange between domestic goods and their foreign counterparts. As a result, changes in the exchange rate have economy-wide implications that are communicated largely through international trade. The effects of exchange rate changes on the economy are particularly important for the APEC region because the exchange rates of its two largest members, the United States and Japan, have experienced large deviations from trend over the past twenty years. The appreciation and subsequent depreciation of the U.S. dollar over the mid-1980s had a significant impact on regional trade linkages, as has the appreciation of the yen since 1993.

In looking at the relationship between real exchange rates (defined as the relative price of goods in different countries) and trade, it is useful to distinguish between the effects of day-to-day exchange rate volatility and more persistent movements in the exchange rate. The breakup of the Bretton Woods fixed exchange rate system in the early 1970s led to the general adoption of floating exchange rates. One consequence of this shift was a marked increase in the level of exchange rate volatility, with day-to-day and month-to-month movements in the exchange rate becoming much larger. For example, the standard deviation of monthly changes in the exchange rate between the yen and the dollar after 1973 has been over triple the value between 1962 and 1972 (Mussa and others, 1994, Table 2). In addition to this short-term volatility, there have also been more persistent deviations of real exchange rates from long-term trends. The most obvious cases are those mentioned earlier: the appreciation and depreciation of the dollar in the mid-1980s and the more recent appreciation of the yen.

This section assesses the impact of both types of exchange rate behavior on trade within the APEC region. The focus will be largely on the impact of medium-term changes in the exchange rate. There is strong evidence that such movements have significant effects on trade; empirical trade equations consistently have found that the real exchange rate is one of the key determinants of both exports and imports. In addition to reviewing the relevant literature, some new estimates of the impact of such exchange rate changes on trade volumes will be presented.

Evidence on the ramifications of short-term exchange rate volatility will also be discussed. Unlike the case for more persistent movements in real exchange rates, studies looking at the effects of exchange rate volatility on trade have come to rather mixed conclusions, with the weight of the evidence pointing to a relatively small impact. This conclusion appears to be fairly robust across different time periods, countries, and statistical techniques. It does, however, contrast with anecdotal evidence that the increase in exchange rate volatility has been a significant concern to people in business.

Patterns of Trade in the APEC Region

The APEC region covers a wide geographic area, including economies from East Asia, Oceania, North America, and, with the recent accession of Chile, South America. Particularly notable from the point of view of analysis is that the region includes much of East Asia, the most economically dynamic region of the world over the past twenty years. The contrast between the rapid economic expansion of this part of the world with the more measured growth of the rest of the APEC region—in particular the more developed economies—provides APEC with a rich set of dynamics that underlie many of the trends in trade.

Table 3-1 shows the rate of growth of real trade in goods and services for the relevant economies during 1973–93, as well as growth in domestic real GDP and a trade-weighted average of real GDP in the economies of trading partners. Both real exports and imports of the economies in the region have grown at over 6 percent a year, over half as much again as trade in the world as a whole. There are significant variations in experience across economies, with the growth in trade being particularly rapid in many of the East Asian countries, in particular the "tigers" (Hong Kong, Korea, Singapore, and Taiwan Province of China), as well as China, Malaysia, Thailand, and Chile. By contrast, the slowest rates of

Table 3-1. Real Growth in Trade of Goods and Services and Output, 1973–93

(Percent a year)

	Exports	Imports	GDP	Trading-Partner GDP[1]
Australia	5.2	4.7	2.8	3.7
Canada	4.5	5.4	2.8	2.5
Chile	9.1	8.1	3.9	2.7
China[2]	11.8	11.8	9.5	—
Hong Kong	16.1	12.9	7.2	3.2
Indonesia	6.1	7.3	6.0	3.8
Japan	6.8	3.4	3.6	3.8
Korea	12.5	11.7	8.2	3.3
Mexico	7.4	5.5	3.6	2.4
Malaysia	10.3	10.2	6.8	4.5
New Zealand	3.9	2.4	1.3	3.1
Papua New Guinea	5.5	2.2	2.8	—
Philippines	5.4	5.5	3.1	3.5
Singapore	9.2	7.9	7.4	4.7
Thailand	12.8	6.6	7.7	3.9
Taiwan Province of China	9.4	10.9	7.8	3.4
United States	5.4	5.3	2.3	3.3
APEC	6.2	6.2	3.8	—
World	4.1[3]	4.1[3]	3.0	—

Source: IMF, World Economic Outlook database and *International Financial Statistics* (various issues). Further details are given in the appendix to Section III.

[1]An export-weighted average of partner-country real GDP in APEC and much of Europe.

[2]1979–93.

[3]Average of exports and imports.

growth have been experienced in the industrial countries within the region (Australia, Canada, Japan, New Zealand, and the United States) as well as the Philippines.

This pattern of rapid expansion in much of East Asia and slower expansion elsewhere, particularly in the industrial countries of the region, also holds for the growth of real GDP. The correspondence between the growth in output and trade should not come as any great surprise, since one of the principal empirical determinants of bilateral trade between countries is the level of output in both countries.[1] It follows that countries whose output is growing rapidly will also experience a speedy expansion of trade. It also follows that bilateral trade will tend to expand fastest with trading partners whose output is also growing rapidly. Because trade tends to be relatively localized (distance is another important determinant of the level of bilateral trade), trade will tend to expand particularly rapidly in regions where all countries are growing rapidly. Some countries in East Asia have benefited from this effect, as can be seen from the data on the growth of output in trading-partner markets, reported in Table 3-1. While the variation in the growth of trading-partner real GDP across economies is much less pronounced than the variation in growth of domestic real GDP, reflecting the diversified nature of external trade, it is clear that in many cases economies with the faster rate of growth of trade also experienced more rapid output growth in destination markets.[2]

The type of goods traded also varies significantly across the APEC region. Figure 3-1 shows the pro-

[1]This is one of the predictions of the gravity model of trade; see Anderson (1979) and Bergstrand (1985). Frankel, Stein, and Wei (1995) provide a discussion of the theoretical underpinnings of the model.

[2]What is less clear is the degree to which the causation may have gone the other way, with the growth in trade stimulating the expansion in output. This issue is beyond the scope of this paper.

Figure 3-1. Proportion of Exports That Are Manufactures
(In percent)

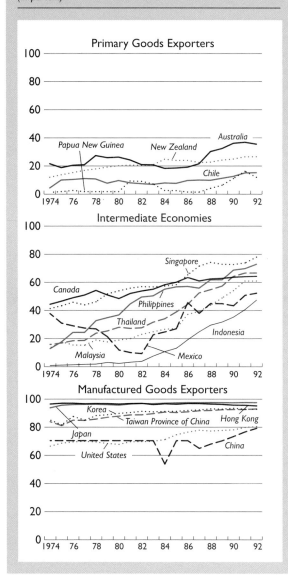

Papua New Guinea, although in the case of Australia there has been some recent expansion in exports of manufactures. At the other end of the scale, the exports of China, Hong Kong, Japan, Korea, Taiwan Province of China, and the United States were heavily concentrated in manufactured goods throughout the period. A number of economies fall into an intermediate category, in which exports were predominantly primary goods at the start of the period but have become more heavily concentrated in manufactured goods over time. This pattern holds for much of East Asia, including Indonesia, Malaysia, the Philippines, Singapore, and Thailand, as well as for Canada and Mexico in North America. This transformation has progressed furthest in Singapore and is most recent in Indonesia, Mexico, and Malaysia.

The composition of imports (Figure 3-2) often shows characteristics opposite to those of exports. For example, Japan is a heavy importer of primary goods, whereas Australia's imports are largely manufactures. In many other economies, however, manufactures make up a high proportion of both exports and imports. In addition, the recent rise in the proportion of exports that are manufactured goods in the intermediate economies has not led to a decrease in the proportion of such imports. Indeed, there appears to have been a slight rise in the proportion of manufactured imports for these countries, as there has for the region as a whole.[4] In short, manufactured goods appear to have been taking up an increased proportion of trade over time, and differences in the composition of imports and exports have been reduced.

The pattern of trade in the 1970s was largely consistent with models that emphasize the importance of differences in resources as a motivation for trade—with natural-resource-rich economies such as Australia and Indonesia specializing in exporting primary goods, and resource-poor economies such as Japan specializing in exporting manufactures. The more recent trend toward high proportions of manufactures in both exports and imports, particularly in the transitional economies, is less consistent with this type of analysis.[5] These recent trends are more compatible with "new" theories of trade, which emphasize that important determinants of the composition of trade include increasing returns to scale and the desire of consumers for product variety. These new theories are able to explain high levels of intra-

portion of merchandise exports (by value), which consist of manufactured goods for each of the economies.[3] There are a number of economies whose trade was heavily concentrated in nonmanufactured goods, which essentially correspond to primary goods. Examples of such primary good exporters include Australia, Chile, New Zealand, and

---

[3]Ratios calculated using volumes of exports show very similar trends to those using values, indicating that the results reflect changes in real behavior rather than movements in relative prices between manufactured and primary goods.

[4]Unlike the case for exports, data on the relevant import volumes are not readily available, so it is not possible to ascertain the degree to which these trends reflect movements in the relative price between primary and manufactured goods.

[5]Note, however, that countries can import and export very different types of goods within the manufacturing sector. For example, China predominantly exports labor-intensive, low-skill products while importing higher-value-added products.

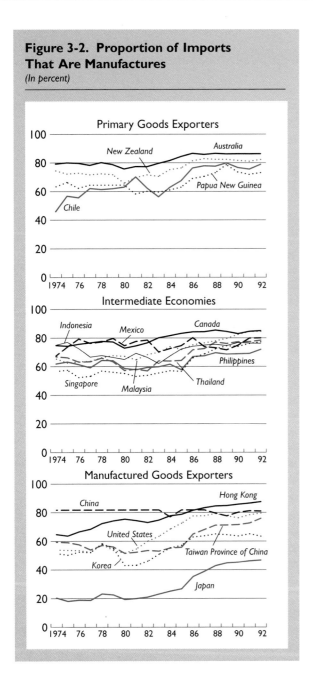

Figure 3-2. Proportion of Imports That Are Manufactures
(In percent)

Primary Goods Exporters

Intermediate Economies

Manufactured Goods Exporters

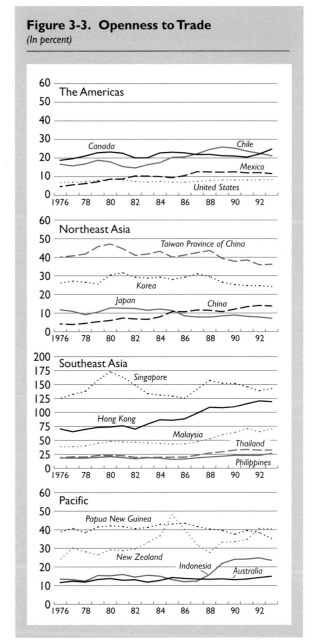

Figure 3-3. Openness to Trade
(In percent)

The Americas

Northeast Asia

Southeast Asia

Pacific

sectoral trade in manufactures, as discussed further below.

The degree of openness of the economies in the APEC region to trade, measured as the average of nominal exports and imports of merchandise as a ratio of domestic output, is shown in Figure 3-3.[6] The two most open economies are Hong Kong and

Singapore, which are centers of entrepôt trade, as is clearly indicated by the fact that average levels of trade often exceed domestic output (note that the panel including Hong Kong and Singapore has a different scale from the others). The recent rapid expansion of both exports and imports as a ratio to output in Malaysia indicates that this country may also be developing this characteristic. At the opposite end of the scale, Japan and the United States, the two largest economies in the region, are also the least open to trade. This reflects a general characteristic that large economies are less open to international

---

[6]Merchandise trade is used because most of the analysis in this section focuses on such trade. The same underlying trends are evident when trade in services is included, although the ratios are somewhat larger.

trade than small ones, presumably reflecting the greater potential within larger economies for intra-national trade, which is not included in the inter-national trade data. In some other economies the ratios have increased rapidly over a limited period, possibly reflecting the impact of trade liberalization. A striking example of this phenomenon is the expansion of trade in China in the 1980s.[7]

There are also important trends within the region as regards intraregional trade. In 1993 approximately two-thirds of all merchandise trade from the APEC region (excluding China, Papua New Guinea, and Brunei Darussalam) went to other economies in this area, up from just over half in 1974.[8] Chile, Hong Kong, and the United States had ratios somewhat below this average (although in the case of Hong Kong this is heavily influenced by the exclusion of China), while Taiwan Province of China and Canada were somewhat above it. The increase in intra-APEC trade largely reflects the rapid economic expansion of many of the Asian members. The proportion of merchandise exports to APEC coming from East Asia[9] increased from around 20 percent in 1974 to over 30 percent in 1993, while that from other economies in the region has remained relatively constant over the same time period.

With the important exception of Japan, the East Asian countries have also generally increased the proportion of APEC exports they receive. The most striking feature of these data, however, is the increase in the proportion of APEC exports going to the United States during the mid-1980s, as the dollar appreciated, and during the subsequent reversal of the appreciation (Figure 3-4). While some of this trend may reflect the path of aggregate demand, the appreciation of the dollar clearly had a significant, if temporary, impact on regional trade patterns. By contrast, the recent appreciation of the yen has not led to the same change, presumably because it has been accompanied by weak domestic demand in Japan.[10]

Bilateral trade patterns show some interesting features, largely revolving around the United States and Japan. Figure 3-5 shows the direction of trade of total exports and imports for seven regions, six within APEC (the United States, Japan, the newly

Figure 3-4. Trade Between the United States and the Rest of the APEC Region
(In percent)

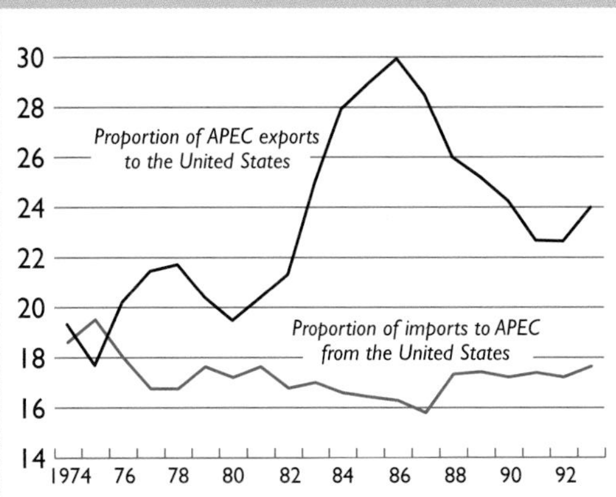

industrializing economies or NIEs,[11] other Asian,[12] Pacific,[13] other Americas[14]) along with non-APEC economies, and Table 3-2 shows the weight of the United States and Japan in 1993 merchandise trade for each economy in the region. Japan's export share is significantly larger than its import share for both the United States and the NIEs, a pattern that is repeated between the NIEs and the United States.[15] Hence, the NIEs generally have a triangular trading relationship, being net importers from Japan and net exporters to the United States. A similar, although less strong, pattern is true of the other Asian economies. By contrast, the Pacific economies have the opposite trilateral arrangement, being net importers from the United States and net exporters to Japan (Table 3-2 indicates this is also true of Chile). Finally, the other American economies have trade that is dominated by bilateral ties with the United States.

The triangular trading relationships of the NIEs, other Asian, and Pacific economies make their economies particularly susceptible to changes in the yen-dollar rate. For example, an appreciation of the yen against the U.S. dollar (compared with trend) generates a rise in the prices of imports compared with prices of exports for those countries that are net

---

[7]Price controls were lifted on many goods around this period, which may also have affected the ratio.

[8]All data come from IMF, *Direction of Trade Statistics* (Washington, various issues). China, Papua New Guinea, and Brunei Darussalam were excluded because their historical data were not reliable. If China, by far the largest of the excluded countries, were included, the proportion of intra-APEC trade in 1993 would rise to just over 70 percent.

[9]Japan, Taiwan Province of China, Korea, Hong Kong, the Philippines, Thailand, Malaysia, Singapore, and Indonesia.

[10]The explanation may also involve J-curves and lags.

[11]Hong Kong, Korea, Singapore, and Taiwan Province of China.

[12]Indonesia, Malaysia, the Philippines, and Thailand.

[13]Australia and New Zealand.

[14]Canada, Chile, and Mexico.

[15]Another interesting feature of the data is the rise in the proportion of U.S. imports coming from Japan and the NIEs in the mid-1980s. Apparently, these economies were particularly benefited by the movement in the exchange rate.

Figure 3-5. Import and Export Weights
(In percent)

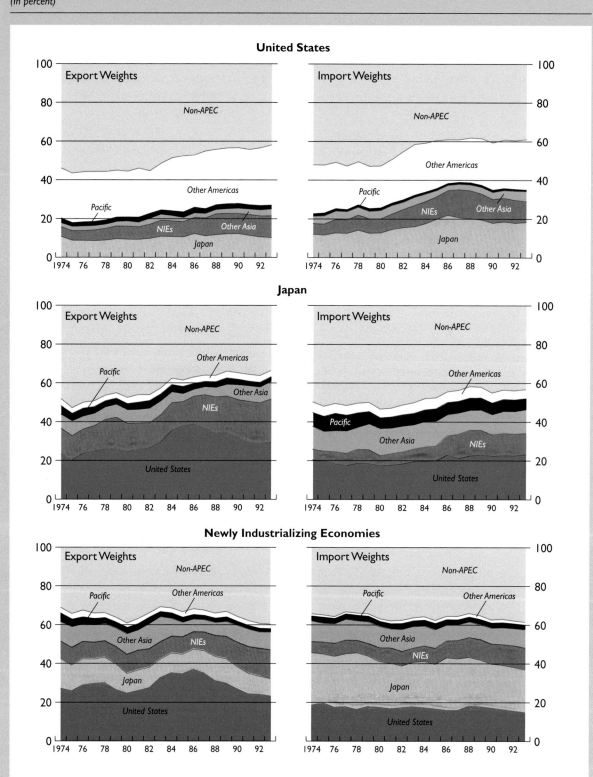

Figure 3-5 (concluded)

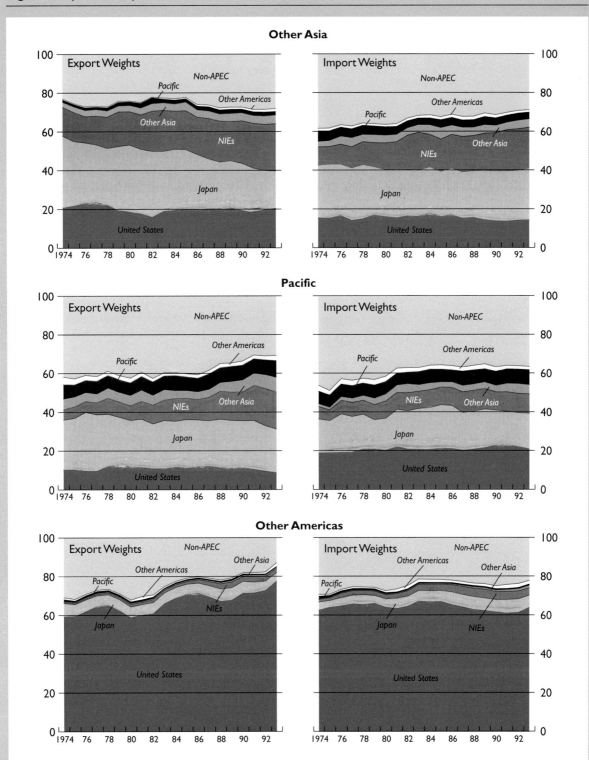

Other Asia

Export Weights

Import Weights

Pacific

Export Weights

Import Weights

Other Americas

Export Weights

Import Weights

Note: NIEs comprise Taiwan Province of China, Korea, Hong Kong, and Singapore. "Other Asia" comprises Thailand, Malaysia, Indonesia, and the Philippines. "Pacific" comprises Australia and New Zealand. "Other Americas" comprises Canada, Mexico, and Chile.

Table 3-2. Weights of United States and Japan in Merchandise Trade in 1993
(In percent of total trade)

	United States		Japan	
	Exports	Imports	Exports	Imports
Australia	8.0	21.5	24.6	19.0
Canada	81.3	65.0	4.6	6.1
Chile	17.3	15.7	22.6	8.0
China	18.5	10.2	17.2	22.5
Hong Kong	23.1	7.3	5.2	16.6
Indonesia	14.2	11.5	30.3	22.1
Japan	29.4	23.2	...	...
Korea	22.7	20.6	14.5	23.0
Mexico	78.5	68.3	2.1	6.5
Malaysia	20.3	16.9	13.0	27.5
New Zealand	11.7	18.0	14.6	16.2
Philippines	38.5	20.0	16.1	22.8
Singapore	20.4	16.3	7.5	21.9
Thailand	21.5	11.7	17.0	30.3
Taiwan Province of China	27.7	21.7	10.6	30.1
United States	...	...	10.3	18.4

Source: Calculated from IMF, *Direction of Trade Statistics* (various issues).

importers from Japan and net exporters to the United States (a depreciation in the yen against the U.S. dollar has the opposite effect).[16] This deterioration in the terms of trade will tend to lower economic welfare in the affected economies, although these effects might be mitigated by an increase in the competitiveness of the countries' exports vis-à-vis Japanese goods in the United States and other markets. In any case, changes in the yen-dollar exchange rate can have important economic implications for other countries in the region.

Trade and the Exchange Rate

Relative Prices

Much of trade theory focuses on underlying reasons for international trade, with relatively limited discussion of the role of the exchange rate either in determining or being determined by these flows. The

factor-proportions theory associated with the names of Heckscher and Ohlin focuses on how differences in factor endowments produce incentives to trade (see Dixit and Norman, 1980, and Jones and Neary, 1985). Countries with, say, large amounts of land and minerals (such as Australia) can be expected to export agricultural goods and commodities, while countries with abundant numbers of people might be expected to trade labor-intensive manufactured goods. Within this approach, the role of the exchange rate is largely limited to the relatively general issue of ensuring that all countries have a comparative advantage in exporting some types of goods.

Although the factor-proportions theory can explain many aspects of trade, it does not explain why much of the trade between industrial countries involves two-way flows of finished manufactured goods (such as cars), which, as discussed earlier, also appear to be becoming more prevalent in the APEC region. This led to the development of the "new" theories of international trade based on increasing returns to scale in production and the desire of consumers for variety in consumption (Krugman, 1980, and Helpman and Krugman, 1985). Increasing returns to scale imply that countries will specialize in the production of different brands of goods within an industry, while the desire of consumers for variety generates demand for foreign brands. The result is international trade in which similar goods are being exchanged in both directions. As in the factor-proportions theory, however, there is relatively little emphasis on the exchange rate or its role in determining trade patterns.[17]

More recently, trade theory has also focused on the behavior of the external balance over time, with the development of the intertemporal approach to the current account.[18] This work emphasizes the role of the external balance in facilitating desirable paths of consumption, saving, and investment across countries. Because these models focus on the appropriate path for net trade over time, and because the real exchange rate is an important determinant of such trade flows, this line of research has implications for the path of the real exchange rate. To date, however, this aspect of the issue appears not to have been studied in any detail, in part because such considerations significantly complicate the analysis.

In contrast to the relative lack of importance of the exchange rate in much of the theoretical work on

---

[16]Bayoumi, Hewitt, and Symansky (1995) includes some welfare calculations for the NIEs from changes in defense spending that illustrate the potential importance of this trilateral trade relationship.

[17]This may change. In particular, with increasing international capital mobility and its implications for the medium-term variability of exchange rates, more attention is beginning to be paid to the impact of exchange rate movements on patterns of trade.

[18]See Sachs (1981) for an early contribution. Obstfeld and Rogoff (forthcoming) contains a survey.

trade, it has played a central role in estimated equations for trade volumes.[19] Trade volumes are usually related to changes in relative prices and to changes in real activity either at home (for imports) or abroad (for exports).[20] For example, in a typical import equation the volume of imports would be related to current and lagged values of the real exchange rate (or the relative price of imports) and of domestic output (or expenditures). Such equations have proven to be highly successful empirically, and they have been consistently used in policy work and macroeconomic models as a way of looking at the impact of the exchange rate on the tradable goods sector.[21] The basic results from this line of work, as summarized by Goldstein and Khan (1985), are that changes in both relative prices and real activity have a significant impact on trade volumes and the nominal trade balance. Their consensus estimates on the negative price elasticity are between ½ and 1 for imports, and somewhat higher (1¼ to 2½) for exports. (These elasticities refer to the prices actually faced by traders, and the elasticities with respect to real exchange rates could well be smaller because of pricing-to-market behavior.) Trade in manufactures appears to have slightly higher elasticities than trade in primary goods, but the differences are not large.

There is, however, a significant difference in the timing of the responses of trade volumes to activity and to relative prices. Although the real activity effect occurs almost immediately, the response of trade volumes to changes in real exchange rates builds more gradually over time. Because a devaluation in the real exchange rate produces an unfavorable terms of trade response, with import prices rising relative to export prices, the initial impact of a fall in the exchange rate on the nominal trade balance can be small or even perverse. The expected effects of the exchange rate on the nominal trade balance may only become clear in the medium term.

Despite their empirical success, these types of equations are not without their critics. The most important concern centers on whether supply terms should also be included in the equations for export volumes, and focuses on the "45-degree rule," which states that there is a one-to-one relationship between estimated elasticities of export demand and growth in home output. Standard export volume equations only take account of demand factors such as the growth of the overseas markets and relative prices. If all economies had the same underlying elasticities with respect to activity, then, with stable real exchange rates, high-growth economies should show a tendency for imports to grow faster than exports, while slow-growing economies should exhibit the opposite characteristic. This differential in the growth of exports and imports would need to be offset by a decline in the real exchange rate of faster-growing economies as consumers are compensated for accepting more goods from these economies.[22] In practice, however, economies with high output growth also have high growth of exports and no decline in their real exchange rates. Instead, estimates of the elasticity on foreign activity are high for high-growth economies and low for low-growth economies—the 45-degree rule (Houthakker and Magee, 1969, and Krugman, 1989). These differences in elasticities mean that export volumes grow at rates similar to those of import volumes in most economies without significant trends in exchange rates.

The close correspondence between estimated activity elasticities for exports and real domestic growth suggests some form of misspecification—a particularly important potential problem for the APEC region, given the wide range of growth experiences within the region. Several authors have suggested that this comes from not including a term measuring domestic supply in the export equation.[23] Such a term can be justified in several ways. For example, in the context of the "new" trade theories it can be argued that, as output expands, so does the number of brands produced by a country. Because consumers desire diversity, this increase in brands generates an increase in demand for exports.[24] Alter-

---

[19]Goldstein and Khan (1985) provided a survey. Two issues that will not be discussed are the pass-through of exchange rates into traded goods prices, in particular pricing-to-market behavior (Krugman, 1987), and so-called "beachhead" effects in which changes in the exchange rate have permanent effects on the trade balance through the fixed costs of entering or leaving a market (Dixit, 1989, and Baldwin and Krugman, 1989).

[20]Some results using this type of specification for APEC economies are reported in the discussion of trade elasticities, below.

[21]Of particular interest from the point of view of the APEC region has been work on the trade deficit in the United States such as Bryant, Holtham, and Hooper (1988) and Krugman (1991), both of whom concluded that real exchange rates are important for trade adjustment.

[22]This discussion ignores the impact of differential productivity growth between traded and nontraded goods on the real exchange rate, generally termed the Balassa-Samuelson effect, discussed in Section II.

[23]An alternative explanation particular to the NIEs, offered by Riedel (1988), is that these economies produce goods that are highly substitutable. Accordingly, the market will accept any amount of goods produced at the going international price, and any deviations from the law of one price reflect statistical discrepancies. This approach, however, fails to explain why trade volumes are found to be connected with deviations from the law of one price in the form of real exchange rate changes.

[24]Krugman (1989). Analogously, the expansion of supply may be correlated with the development of higher-quality products at prices that lead to an increase in the demand for exports.

natively, in a more traditional demand and supply framework, the addition of a supply term involves relaxing the assumption that supply is perfectly elastic that is used to identify the export equation.

There are by now a number of estimates of export equations that include supply terms in them, including several for APEC economies.[25] The results from this estimation have been relatively successful, to the extent that such terms are often significant. More important from the point of view of this discussion, estimates of price elasticities using this specification are generally similar to those produced by traditional export equations. Hence, the issue of the 45-degree rule does not appear to be of central importance in estimating price elasticities of trade.

Exchange Rate Volatility

The connection between exchange rate volatility and trade has also been examined in some detail, particularly in the early part of the period of floating exchange rates.[26] These analyses can be conveniently divided into those that use time-series evidence to look at the relationship between volatility and trade and those that use cross-sectional comparisons across countries.

Much of the time-series evidence has started from the types of empirical models of trade volumes discussed above. The impact of exchange rate volatility is then measured by adding a term representing this volatility into the equation. The results from these studies have varied quite widely. A few have found significant effects from the volatility term, but most have found little or no impact (see the surveys in IMF, 1984, and more recently in Commission of the European Communities, 1990). The theoretical issues involved are discussed in Gagnon (1993), who used a model of international trade to estimate the likely impact of increased exchange rate volatility. He found that higher volatility has a small negative impact on trade volumes, with the rise in volatility after the Bretton Woods period lowering trade by only 1–3 percent, which may help to explain the ambiguity of the empirical results.

An alternative approach is to compare behavior across countries, rather than over time. Again, a model of expected trade flows between countries is used to calculate expected trade volumes between these countries, with a term representing exchange rate volatility added. Frankel and Wei (1993) carried out such a test using a large set of data on bilateral

trade between 63 industrial and developing economies (implying almost 2,000 bilateral flows), including many members of APEC. The large number of observations enabled them to estimate a highly significant coefficient on exchange rate volatility. However, as in the case of Gagnon's theoretical work, the implied impact was relatively small. For example, a doubling of the level of the real exchange rate variability in Europe in 1990 (which would have returned such variability to its 1980 level, before attempts to control such volatility through the exchange rate mechanism of the European Monetary System) would have lowered intraregional trade volumes by only 0.7 percent.

Overall, the evidence appears to point to a small direct effect of exchange rate volatility on trade volumes. At the same time, this observation appears at odds with concerns often expressed by business people about floating exchange rates. One explanation for this may be that higher short-term volatility has been associated with larger, and more persistent, exchange rate misalignments, and that these misalignments clearly involve substantial costs and can increase protectionist pressures. Another is that in many cases floating exchange rates may have been associated with more unstable macroeconomic policies. Such indirect influences, which are unlikely to be captured in econometric studies that relate exchange rate volatility to trade volumes, may also help to explain the dichotomy between the empirical evidence and the widespread concerns about exchange rate volatility among policymakers.

Estimated APEC Trade Elasticities

This part of the section reports some new estimates of trade equations for the APEC economies to supplement the work on exchange rate elasticities discussed above. Standard empirical specifications are used because attempts to include domestic supply in the export equations were not successful. Equations are estimated for 15 APEC economies (China, Papua New Guinea, and Brunei Darussalam were excluded because of lack of data).

Annual data on real merchandise exports and imports from 1974 through 1993 were regressed on the real effective exchange rate for the economy in question (defined using consumer prices across countries) plus the growth in real GDP of partner countries (for exports) or of real domestic GDP (for imports).[27] The

---

[25]For example, Helkie and Hooper (1988) for the United States and Muscatelli and Stevenson (1995) for NIEs.

[26]The earlier literature was surveyed in International Monetary Fund (1984).

[27]Annual data were used because quarterly data were not available for many of these economies. No attempt was made to look at different types of goods, such as manufactures and primary goods, separately.

Table 3-3. Estimated Activity Elasticities

	Exports		Imports	
	Short-run	Long-run	Short-run	Long-run
Panel of all countries	1.88**	1.96**	1.95**	1.46**
Australia	0.04	1.33**	1.77**	1.85**
Canada	2.22**	2.06**	1.99**	2.01**
Chile	2.04*	2.87**	1.53**	1.70**
Hong Kong	2.98*	4.11**	1.76**	1.92**
Indonesia	1.03	1.27	−0.27	1.66**
Japan	1.73**	2.10**	2.11	0.79**
Korea	4.90**	3.12**	1.61	1.36**
Mexico	−0.05	1.55	1.16	1.60**
Malaysia	2.14	1.86**	3.06**	1.47**
New Zealand	1.51	0.98**	0.78	1.70**
Philippines	2.15	1.34**	2.09**	1.65**
Singapore	3.52**	1.77**	2.89**	1.05**
Thailand	3.28*	2.73**	3.93**	1.03**
Taiwan Province of China	2.70**	3.28**	0.94	1.23**
United States	0.65	1.47**	3.29**	2.46**

Note: See the appendix to Section III for details of the regressions. One and two asterisks indicate that the coefficient is significant at the 5 and 1 percent levels, respectively.

real exchange rate was used, rather than a more direct estimate of relative prices of traded goods, because it provides a more direct link between exchange rate changes and trade. A standard error-correction estimation procedure was adopted in which the long-run elasticities were first estimated using an equation that included only levels of exports (imports), the real exchange rate, and partner-country (domestic) real GDP. Next, the short-run elasticities were estimated from a dynamic equation using the rate of change of the variables plus the residuals from the levels equation (the "error-correction term").

Details of the data, specification, estimation technique, and parameter estimates are given in the appendix to this section. To gain more of an idea of "average" behavior across all countries, a panel regression was run, in which the data across all countries were combined and used to estimate a single regression. Such a regression is a useful way of summarizing the characteristics of the data, given the relatively limited number of data points (20) per economy and the consequent lack of precision of many of the estimated coefficients associated with individual regressions. Note, however, that tests showed that the assumption that the estimated coefficients are equal across all countries is rejected, implying significant variation in behavior across individual economies.

Table 3-3 reports the estimated short- and long-run elasticities with respect to output and the real exchange rate.[28] Panel estimates indicated similar activity elasticities for both exports and imports, with the short-run elasticity being around 2 and the long-run value being similar for exports and about 1½ for imports. The size and importance of activity effects in determining real trade are confirmed by the estimates for individual economies. The vast majority of both short- and long-run elasticities are estimated at over 1. The long-run export elasticities show clear evidence of the 45-degree rule, with fast-growing economies such as Hong Kong, Korea, and Taiwan Province of China having estimated activity elasticities of over 3, while slower-growing and more mature economies such as Australia, New Zealand, and the United States have relatively low values.

The results for short- and long-run real exchange rate elasticities (Table 3-4) were more mixed than those for activity, as is typical in the literature. In the case of exports the panel estimation yielded a short-run elasticity of −0.18, which rose to −0.80 in the long run, indicating a significant increase in the elas-

---

[28]The long-run elasticities are best thought of as representing the likely impact of sustained medium-term deviations from trend, not as reflecting the impact of long-term trends in the real exchange rate.

Table 3-4. Estimated Real Exchange Rate Elasticities

	Exports		Imports	
	Short-run	Long-run	Short-run	Long-run
Panel of all countries	−0.18**	−0.80**	0.26**	0.28
Australia	−0.31	−0.19	0.21	0.45**
Canada	0.15	0.00	0.23	0.49
Chile	−0.45	0.10	0.44	0.23*
Hong Kong	0.02	−0.07	0.32	1.01**
Indonesia	−0.16	−0.32	0.63**	0.68**
Japan	−0.23*	−0.69**	−0.03	0.55
Korea	−0.41	−0.52	0.27	0.61
Mexico	−0.16	−0.77	1.23**	1.43**
Malaysia	−0.06	−0.53	0.24	0.01
New Zealand	−0.05	−0.51	−0.20	0.68
Philippines	0.06	0.10	−0.01	−0.75
Singapore	0.52	−0.21	0.07	0.00
Thailand	−0.09	−0.99	2.14**	0.75
Taiwan Province of China	−0.04	−0.70*	0.32	0.66
United States	−0.28*	−0.86**	0.05	0.26**

Note: See the appendix to Section III for details of the regressions. One and two asterisks indicate that the coefficient is significant at the 5 and 1 percent levels, respectively.

ticity over time. The results for individual countries were generally correctly signed and rose over time but, except in the case of the United States and Japan, were rarely significant at conventional levels. The price elasticities on imports were again generally correctly signed, rose over time, but were rarely significant at conventional levels. Unlike the export regressions, however, the individual estimates tended to be larger than the panel results. This was particularly true of the long-run estimates, where the median value of the individual economy estimates (0.55) was almost double the (insignificant) panel estimate of 0.28.

One reason for the lack of precision of the real exchange rate elasticities may be the impact of factors such as changes in trade policy or shifts in the type of goods being traded, which may be of particular importance for many of the economies in the APEC region. Such shifts may obscure the true relationship between real exchange rates and trade. It is notable that the estimates for economies such as the United States and Japan, which are least likely to experience such shifts because of the relative stability of their trade regimes, are generally better determined than those for many of the faster-growing developing nations. Another potential source of problems is the use of consumer price indices in the calculation of the real exchange rate. These indices, which were adopted because of their wide availabil-

ity, include nontraded goods; thus, although they correspond to movements in overall relative prices across economies, they do not necessarily correspond closely to relative prices of goods that are traded. Finally, the use of aggregate data on trade may obscure differences in behavior across different types of goods, such as manufactures and primary commodities.

Overall, the standard empirical model of trade appears to work fairly well for the APEC region, a conclusion that is supported by similar work on the region by others.[29] At the same time, the small estimated elasticities on the real exchange rate indicate a degree of elasticity pessimism, which is again not an unusual result from this type of estimation for developing countries.[30] In summary, sustained exchange rate changes appear to have significant, if somewhat muted, effects on trade within the APEC region.

---

[29]Estimates for the industrial countries in the region abound. For example, Masson, Symansky, and Meredith (1990) provided estimates for the United States, Japan, and Canada. Results using various specifications for exports of several NIEs can be found in Arize (1990).

[30]Reinhart (1995) came to a very similar conclusion. As noted earlier, the Goldstein and Khan (1985) elasticities reflect transaction prices, which will tend to be larger than those from real exchange rates, owing to pricing-to-market behavior.

Table 3-5. Effect of Major Regional Currencies on Trade in the APEC Region
(Percent change)

	10 Percent Real Appreciation Against the U.S. Dollar			10 Percent Real Appreciation Against the Japanese Yen		
	Exports	Imports	Real net trade/GDP[1]	Exports	Imports	Real net trade/GDP[1]
Australia	−0.14	0.56	−0.11	−0.44	0.49	−0.14
Canada	−1.46	1.69	−0.78	−0.08	0.16	−0.06
Chile	−0.31	0.41	−0.15	−0.41	0.21	−0.13
Hong Kong	−0.42	0.19	−0.72	−0.09	0.43	−0.63
Indonesia	−0.26	0.30	−0.13	−0.55	0.57	−0.26
Korea	−0.41	0.54	−0.23	−0.26	0.60	−0.21
Mexico	−1.41	1.78	−0.38	−0.04	0.17	−0.03
Malaysia	−0.37	0.44	−0.56	−0.23	0.72	−0.65
New Zealand	−0.21	0.47	−0.27	−0.26	0.42	−0.27
Philippines	−0.69	0.52	−0.31	−0.29	0.59	−0.25
Singapore	−0.37	0.42	−1.13	−0.14	0.57	−1.03
Thailand	−0.39	0.30	−0.22	−0.31	0.79	−0.37
Taiwan Province of China	−0.50	0.56	−0.38	−0.19	0.78	−0.34

Note: See the text for an explanation of the calculations.
[1] As a percentage of real GDP.

Impact of Changes in Bilateral Exchange Rates on Trade

Given the large differences in openness and the importance of trilateral trading relationships in the APEC region, it is of interest to consider the likely impact on trade of changes in the dollar and the yen, the two key currencies in the region. This section provides some highly stylized estimates of the impact of bilateral changes between the dollar and the yen on the one hand and other regional currencies on the other. The calculation uses 1993 values for openness and direction of trade and assumes a real exchange rate elasticity for export volumes of −0.18, the short-run value estimated using the panel data set. The real exchange rate elasticity for real imports is likewise set to 0.26, the estimated value using the panel data. As discussed earlier, long-run effects are likely to be significantly larger.

The effects of a 10 percent appreciation against the dollar and the yen on real exports, real imports, and real net trade as a percentage of GDP (which provides an estimate of the overall impact on activity) are reported in Table 3-5. Note that the impact on the nominal trade balance will be smaller than that on real net trade because changes in prices will partially offset the change in volumes. In addition, it should be recalled that the results refer to a real exchange rate appreciation. To the extent that nominal exchange rate movements cause offsetting movements in domestic prices, the effects of nominal exchange rate changes will be smaller.

The economies of the region can be divided into three categories.[31] Canada and Mexico are relatively sensitive to changes in the real value of the U.S. dollar while being fairly insulated from movements in the yen. The extremely open economies of Hong Kong, Singapore, and Malaysia are also highly sensitive to changes in the dollar and are almost equally influenced by changes in the real value of the yen. Finally, the vast majority of economies in the region are dependent on both exchange rates, but to a rather lesser extent than Hong Kong, Malaysia, and Singapore.

These results are intended only to be illustrative. Different assumptions about trade elasticities would give different results. To take just one example, it is very possible that Japan's exports to East Asian economies, which are often heavily skewed toward investment goods, may be relatively insensitive to changes in exchange rates. The calculations also take no account of third-country effects. As the exchange rate against, say, the dollar appreciates, economies

---

[31] Results for the United States and Japan are not reported because they would depend on whether the appreciation was general across all countries or specific to a few.

may seek out new markets to replace the lower demand for exports coming from the United States.

At the same time, Table 3-5 does illustrate two general features of the APEC region. The first is the universal importance of the United States in the trade of other countries. The second is the similar importance of Japan in the trade of those economies in Asia and the Pacific.

Concluding Perspectives

There has been a steady increase over time in the importance of the intra-APEC component of overall international trade in the region, and in the proportion of manufactured goods within merchandise trade. Both of these trends largely reflect robust growth in East Asia. Another feature of some parts of the region is triangular trading relationships with the two largest economies in the region, the United States and Japan. This is particularly true of the East Asian economies, which tend to be net importers from Japan and net exporters to the United States.

The available evidence indicates that higher exchange rate volatility has little direct influence on regional trade flows. By contrast, sustained deviations in the exchange rate from trend (which may be more likely to occur in a situation of higher volatility) do have a significant impact on trade volumes, although the elasticities estimated in this study were on the lower end of existing estimates. Illustrative simulations indicate that all of the economies in the region are significantly affected by changes in the value of the U.S. dollar, while the Japanese exchange rate plays a similar role for those APEC economies not in the Americas.

In short, with the exception of the immediate neighbors of the United States, movements in both of the major regional currencies can have a significant impact on trade and activity for other countries in the region. The trilateral trading pattern of many of these economies further complicates this situation, because movements in the bilateral rate of the dollar against the yen also create changes in their external terms of trade. Such a situation creates significant complications for policymakers when the bilateral exchange rate between the dollar and the yen shows a significant divergence from its long-term trend, as occurred in the mid-1980s with the appreciation and subsequent depreciation of the dollar.

Appendix: Estimation of the Trade Equations

Annual data from 1974–93 on real merchandise exports, real merchandise imports, real GDP, real GDP of partner countries, and real effective exchange rates were collected for APEC economies (except China, Papua New Guinea, and Brunei Darussalam, which were excluded for data reasons). Exports, imports, and real GDP were generally collected from the IMF's World Economic Outlook database, although in some cases data from the IMF's *International Financial Statistics* were used. The real effective exchange rates were based on IMF estimates calculated using consumer price indices for a wide range of developing and industrial countries, reported in *International Financial Statistics*. Owing to limitations in availability of historical consumer prices for some developing countries, only a subset of the countries used in the official IMF calculations was included, with only those countries with weights of 1 percent or greater in the original IMF calculations being used.[32] Finally, the real GDP of partner countries was calculated using an export-weighted combination of the real GDP of other countries in the region and most European economies.

Dickey-Fuller tests of the data indicated that in the vast majority of cases the logarithms of real exports, real imports, real GDP, real GDP in partner countries, and real effective exchange rates were nonstationary, whereas their first differences were stationary.[33] Accordingly, a three-step estimation procedure suggested by Engle and Yoo, as described in Cuthbertson, Hall, and Taylor (1992), was adopted. It is a simple adaption of the standard two-step procedure suggested by Engle and Granger (1987) in which the initial parameter estimates of the long-run relationship (the cointegrating vector) were used to add an error-correction term to the second-stage dynamic equation. The third stage involved a further level of regression whose results were used to improve the efficiency of the first-stage parameter estimates and to provide standard errors for these coefficients. This is useful because the coefficients from the first-stage regression have nonstandard distributions, so that statistical significance cannot be calculated using the estimated standard errors.

In the first step the logarithm of exports (imports) was regressed on the real exchange rate and partner-

---

[32]Experiments with real effective exchange rates based on separate export and import weights produced very similar results. Despite the importance of trilateral trading patterns in many countries, the different weights on exports and imports made relatively little difference to the empirical results.

[33]Details of these tests are available from the author. In the case of Mexico, exports and real GDP were not found to be stationary even in first differences. Similarly, in the Philippines first differences of imports and real GDP did not appear to be stationary. More marginal failures occurred in the cases of the first differences of real exchange rates for Malaysia, Singapore, and the United States; real GDP in New Zealand and Thailand; and real exports for the United States.

country (domestic) GDP. Specifically, the following regressions were run using ordinary least squares:

$$\ln(X_t) = \alpha_X + \beta_X \ln(E_t) + \Psi_X \ln(YF_t) + \varepsilon_{Xt}$$
$$\ln(M_t) = \alpha_M + \beta_M \ln(E_t) + \Psi_M \ln(Y_t) + \varepsilon_{Mt}, \quad (3\text{-}1)$$

where $X, M, E, YF,$ and Y represent real exports, real imports, the real effective exchange rate, partner-country GDP, and domestic GDP, respectively.

The coefficients β and Ψ represent initial estimates of the long-run elasticities with respect to the real exchange rate and output. The next step in the estimation was to estimate a dynamic equation involving the first differences of the explanatory variables plus the lagged residuals from the first-stage estimation, the "error-correction term."[34] Specifically, the following regressions were estimated:

$$\Delta\ln(X_t) = \delta_X + \phi_X \Delta\ln(E_t) + \eta_X \Delta\ln(YF_t)$$
$$+ \kappa_X \varepsilon_{Xt-1} + \varepsilon'_{Xt}$$
$$\Delta\ln(M_t) = \delta_M + \phi_M \Delta\ln(E_t) + \eta_M \Delta\ln(Y_t) \quad (3\text{-}2)$$
$$+ \kappa_M \varepsilon_{Mt-1} + \varepsilon'_{Mt}.$$

The coefficients ϕ and η represent the short-run elasticities with respect to the real effective exchange rate and activity, respectively, and κ, the coefficient on the error-correction term, specifies the speed with which the system tends to the long-run equilibrium. Specifically, the mean lag of the adjustment process is equal to $-1/\kappa$, so that the larger is the value of κ in absolute terms, the faster is the rate of adjustment to long-run equilibrium.

The third stage involved regressing the residuals of the second-stage regressions on the level of the real exchange rate and activity, this time multiplied by the negative of the coefficient on the error-correction term, κ. The coefficients from this third stage were added to the initial parameter estimates from the first stage to provide the final estimates of the long-run coefficients, with the standard errors from this third-stage regression representing the standard errors of these adjusted coefficients. In a few cases this adjustment equation caused the coefficient on the real effective exchange rate to become perverse. This was generally associated with small and insignificant estimates of the error-correction parameter, κ, used to calculate data for the third-stage regression. In these cases the parameter estimates from the original first-stage levels regression were reported.

To gain more of an idea of "average" behavior across all countries, a panel regression was also calculated, in which the data across all countries were combined and used to estimate a single regression. Tests showed that the assumption that the estimated coefficients are equal across all countries is rejected, implying significant variation in behavior across individual economies. Because the stacking of the data meant that a much larger number of observations were involved in the regression (300, as opposed to 20 in the individual regressions), the two-step estimation procedure was dispensed with and equations (3-1) and (3-2) were combined into a single regression:

$$\Delta X_t = \xi + \phi_X \Delta E_t + \beta'_X E_{t-1} + \eta_X \Delta YF_t$$
$$+ \Psi'_X YF_{t-1} + \kappa_X X_{t-1}$$
$$\Delta M_t = \xi + \phi_M \Delta E_t + \beta'_M E_{t-1} + \eta_M \Delta Y_t \quad (3\text{-}3)$$
$$+ \Psi'_M Y_{t-1} + \kappa_M M_{t-1},$$

where $\beta' = \beta * \kappa$ and $\Psi' = \Psi * \kappa$.

Regression results for exports are reported in Table 3-6; Table 3-7 reports the same information for imports. The long-run elasticities on activity for exports are large and generally highly significant. The estimate from the panel regression is 1.96, while the estimates for the individual countries vary from just under 1 in the case of New Zealand to slightly over 4 for Hong Kong. Almost all are significant at the 1 percent level. The impact of the 45-degree rule can be clearly seen in the data, with fast-growing economies such as Hong Kong, Korea, and Taiwan Province of China having estimated activity elasticities of over 3, while slower-growing and more mature economies such as Australia, New Zealand, and the United States have relatively low values. The short-run activity elasticities from the panel regression are well determined and very similar to their long-run counterparts. The estimated short-run activity elasticities for individual economies are for the most part similar in magnitude to their long-run counterparts but are generally less well-determined.

The estimated short- and long-run elasticities on the real effective exchange rate from the panel regression for exports are both highly significant, with the estimated elasticity rising from -0.18 to -0.80 over time. The most successful individual country regressions are for the United States and Japan, the two largest economies in the region, which show a pattern similar to the panel results. By contrast, although the price elasticities on the other individual regressions are generally correctly signed, they are rarely significant at conventional levels in either the short run or the long run. They also tend to be smaller in absolute value than the panel results. Finally, the terms on the error-correction terms indi-

---

[34]These errors need to be stationary for the procedure to be valid. Formal Dickey-Fuller tests rarely indicated that nonstationarity could be rejected for these terms. However, the coefficients on the lagged level of the residual were often large, indicating that there was significant mean-reverting behavior. Given the known lack of power of Dickey-Fuller tests in small samples, the estimation was continued.

Table 3-6. Export Regression Results

	Long-Run Elasticities		Short-Run Elasticities		
	Output	Real exchange rate	Output	Real exchange rate	Error-Correction Term
Panel of all countries	1.96**	−0.80**	1.88**	−0.18**	−0.09**
Australia	1.33**	−0.19	0.04	−0.31	−0.50*
Canada	2.06**	0.00	2.22**	0.15	−0.33
Chile	2.87**	0.10	2.04*	−0.45	−0.45
Hong Kong	4.11**	−0.07	2.98*	0.02	−0.72**
Indonesia	1.27	−0.32	1.03	−0.16	−0.24
Japan	2.10**	−0.69**	1.73**	−0.23*	−0.55**
Korea	3.12**	−0.52	4.90**	−0.41	−0.58**
Mexico	1.55	−0.77	−0.05	−0.16	−0.10
Malaysia	1.86**	−0.53	2.14	−0.06	−0.53*
New Zealand	0.98**	−0.51	1.51*	−0.05	−0.74**
Philippines	1.34**	0.10	2.15	0.06	−0.42
Singapore	1.77**	−0.21	3.52**	0.52	−0.48
Thailand	2.73**	−0.99	3.28*	−0.09	−0.36
Taiwan Province of China	3.28**	−0.70*	2.70**	−0.04	−0.83**
United States	1.47**	−0.85**	0.65	−0.28*	−0.59**

Note: The text describes how the elasticities were calculated. One and two asterisks indicate that the coefficient is significant at the 5 and 1 percent levels of significance, respectively.

Table 3-7. Import Regression Results

	Long-Run Elasticities		Short-Run Elasticities		
	Output	Real exchange rate	Output	Real exchange rate	Error-Correction Term
Panel of all countries	1.46**	0.28**	1.95**	0.26**	−0.20
Australia	1.85**	0.45**	1.77**	0.21	−1.11**
Canada[1]	2.01**	0.49	1.99**	0.23	−0.15
Chile	1.70**	0.23*	1.53**	0.44	−0.86**
Hong Kong[1]	1.92**	1.01**	1.76**	0.32	−0.12
Indonesia	1.66**	0.68**	−0.27	0.63**	−1.00**
Japan	0.79**	0.55	2.11	−0.03	−0.31
Korea	1.36**	0.61	1.61	0.27	−0.22
Mexico	1.60**	1.43**	1.16	1.23**	−0.13
Malaysia[1]	1.47**	0.01	3.06**	0.24	−0.36
New Zealand	1.70**	0.68	0.78	−0.20	−0.43*
Philippines	1.65**	−0.75	2.09**	−0.01	−0.25
Singapore	1.05**	0.00	2.89**	0.07	−0.43*
Thailand	1.03**	0.75	3.93**	2.14**	−0.45*
Taiwan Province of China[1]	1.23**	0.66	0.94	0.32	−0.34
United States	2.46**	0.26**	3.29**	0.05	−0.82**

Note: The text describes how the elasticities were calculated. One and two asterisks indicate that the coefficient is significant at the 5 and 1 percent levels of significance, respectively.

[1]The Engle-Yoo procedure was not used in these cases.

cate that the mean lag in these regressions generally appears reasonable, of the order of two years or so.

The results for the import equations are in many respects similar to those for the export equations. The activity elasticities tend to be large and well determined, particularly in the long run, where all of the estimates are significant at the 1 percent significance level. The range of estimated long-run elasticities is also somewhat smaller than in the case of the export elasticities, as might be expected given the absence of the problem posed by the 45-degree rule.

The price elasticities are again generally correctly signed but rarely significant at conventional levels. Unlike the export regressions, however, the individual estimates tend to be larger than the panel results. This is particularly true of the long-run estimates, where at 0.55 the median value of the individual economy estimates is almost double the (insignificant) panel estimate of 0.28. Finally, although many of the individual economy error-correction terms show reasonable adjustment speeds, some of them indicate surprisingly fast or slow responses.

To summarize, the output elasticities are generally large and well determined. By contrast, the price elasticities are less well-determined and generally quite low. Hence, although there is considerable evidence that real exchange rates do effect trade volumes in the expected directions, the results are quite pessimistic as regards the size of the underlying elasticities.

References

Anderson, James E., 1979, "A Theoretical Foundation for the Gravity Equation," *American Economic Review*, Vol. 69 (March), pp. 106–16.

Arize, Augustine, 1990, "An Econometric Evaluation of Export Behavior in Seven Asian Developing Countries," *Applied Economics*, Vol. 22 (July), pp. 891–904.

Baldwin, Richard, and Paul R. Krugman, 1989, "Persistent Trade Effects of Large Exchange Rate Shocks," *Quarterly Journal of Economics*, Vol. 104 (November), pp. 635–54.

Bayoumi, Tamim, Daniel Hewitt, and Steven Symansky, 1995, "MULTIMOD Simulations of the Effects on Developing Countries of Decreasing Military Spending," in *North-South Linkages and International Macroeconomic Policy*, ed. by David Vines and David Currie (Cambridge and New York: Cambridge University Press).

Bergstrand, J.H., 1985, "The Gravity Equation in International Trade: Some Microeconomic Foundations and Empirical Evidence," *Review of Economics and Statistics*, Vol. 67 (August), pp. 474–81.

Bryant, Ralph C., Gerald Holtham, and Peter Hooper, eds., 1988, *External Deficits and the Dollar: The Pit and the Pendulum* (Washington: Brookings Institution).

Commission of the European Communities, 1990, "One Market, One Money: An Evaluation of the Potential Benefits and Costs of Forming an Economic and Monetary Union," *European Economy*, No. 44 (October), pp. 3–347.

Cuthbertson, Keith, Stephen G. Hall, and Mark P. Taylor, 1992, *Applied Econometric Techniques* (Ann Arbor: University of Michigan Press).

Dixit, Avinash, 1989, "Hysteresis, Import Penetration, and Exchange Rate Passthrough," *Quarterly Journal of Economics*, Vol. 104 (May), pp. 205–28.

Dixit, Avinash, and Victor D. Norman, 1980, *Theory of International Trade: A Dual, General Equilibrium Approach* (Cambridge and New York: Cambridge University Press).

Engle, R.F., and C.W.J. Granger, 1987, "Co-Integration and Error Correction: Representation, Estimation, and Testing," *Econometrica*, Vol. 55 (March), pp. 251–76.

Frankel, Jeffrey, and Shang-jin Wei, 1993, "Trade Blocs and Currency Blocs," NBER Working Paper 4335 (Cambridge, Mass.: National Bureau of Economic Research, April).

Frankel, Jeffrey, Ernesto Stein, and Shang-jin Wei, 1995, "Trading Blocs and the Americas: The Natural, the Unnatural, and the Super-Natural," *Journal of Development Economics*, Vol. 47 (June), pp. 61–95.

Gagnon, Joseph E., 1993, "Exchange Rate Variability and the Level of International Trade," *Journal of International Economics*, Vol. 34 (May), pp. 269–87.

Goldstein, Morris, and Mohsin S. Khan, 1985, "Income and Price Elasticities in Trade," in *Handbook of International Economics*, Vol. 1, ed. by Ronald W. Jones and Peter B. Kenen (Amsterdam: North-Holland).

Helkie, William L., and Peter Hooper, 1988, "An Empirical Analysis of the External Deficit, 1980–86," in *External Deficits and the Dollar: The Pit and the Pendulum*, ed. by Ralph C. Bryant, Gerald Holtham, and Peter Hooper (Washington: Brookings Institution).

Helpman, Elhanan, and Paul R. Krugman, 1985, *Market Structure and Foreign Trade* (Cambridge, Mass.: MIT Press).

Houthakker, H.S., and Stephen P. Magee, 1969, "Income and Price Elasticities in World Trade," *Review of Economics and Statistics*, Vol. 51, pp. 111–24.

International Monetary Fund, 1984, *Exchange Rate Volatility and World Trade*, Occasional Paper 28 (Washington: International Monetary Fund, July).

Jones, Ronald W., and J. Peter Neary, 1985, "The Positive Theory of International Trade," in *Handbook of International Economics*, Vol. 1, ed. by Ronald W. Jones and Peter B. Kenen (Amsterdam: North-Holland).

Krugman, Paul R., 1980, "Scale Economies, Product Differentiation, and the Pattern of Trade," *American Economic Review*, Vol. 70, pp. 950–59.

———, 1987, "Pricing to Market When the Exchange Rate Changes," in *Real-Financial Linkages Among Open Economies*, ed. by Sven W. Arndt and J.D. Richardson (Cambridge, Mass.: MIT Press).

————, 1989, "Differences in Income Elasticities and Trends in Real Exchange Rates," *European Economic Review*, Vol. 33 (May), pp. 1031–54.

————, 1991, *Has the Adjustment Process Worked?* Policy Analyses in International Economics, No. 34 (Washington: Institute for International Economics).

Masson, Paul, Steven Symansky, and Guy Meredith, 1990, *MULTIMOD Mark II: A Revised and Extended Model*, Occasional Paper 71 (Washington: International Monetary Fund, July).

Muscatelli, Vito Antonio, and Andrew A. Stevenson, 1995, "Modeling Aggregate Manufactured Exports for Some Asian Newly Industrializing Economies," *Review of Economics and Statistics*, Vol. 77 (February), pp. 147–55.

Mussa, Michael, Morris Goldstein, Peter B. Clark, Donald J. Mathieson, and Tamim Bayoumi, 1994, *Improving the International Monetary System: Constraints and Possibilities*, Occasional Paper 116 (Washington: International Monetary Fund, December).

Obstfeld, Maurice, and Kenneth S. Rogoff, forthcoming, "The Intertemporal Approach to the Current Account," in *Handbook of International Economics*, ed. by Gene Grossman and Kenneth Rogoff (Amsterdam: North-Holland).

Riedel, James, 1988, "The Demand for LDC Exports of Manufactures: Estimates from Hong Kong," *Economic Journal*, Vol. 98 (March), pp. 138–48.

Reinhart, Carmen M., 1995, "Devaluation, Relative Prices, and International Trade: Evidence from Developing Countries," *Staff Papers*, International Monetary Fund, Vol. 42 (June), pp. 290–312.

Sachs, Jeffrey D., 1981, "The Current Account and Macroeconomic Adjustment in the 1970s," *Brookings Papers on Economic Activity: 1*, pp. 201–68.

IV Foreign Direct Investment and the Exchange Rate

Tamim Bayoumi, Leonardo Bartolini, and Michael Klein

Foreign direct investment (FDI) represents the acquisition by foreign residents of a controlling claim on firms (through equity) or on real estate, or further investment in an enterprise so controlled.[1] It is the word "controlling" that distinguishes FDI from foreign portfolio investment, the other subcategory of private foreign investment.[2] The *System of National Accounts*[3] considers that a foreign investor controls a corporation or other asset if it owns 10 percent or more of the particular enterprise, rather lower than the 51 percent that is usually associated with the definition of a controlling interest.[4] FDI itself is often divided into two further categories: mergers and acquisitions, in which an existing concern is bought; and "greenfield" investment, in which the enterprise is started from scratch.

Among the different components of FDI, acquisition of existing assets has been the predominant mechanism for making direct investments in industrial countries in recent decades (comprising, for instance, 80 percent of FDI in the United States). Even Japanese firms, which have historically displayed an inclination toward greenfield investment and joint ventures, have increasingly sought to expand through acquisitions in recent years (Kester, 1991; Froot, 1991; and Harris and Ravenscraft, 1991).

In either case, FDI includes a variety of transactions, such as the purchase of stock, the creation of production facilities or of distribution networks, and the acquisition of land for commercial or residential use. Because of the growing importance of these transactions, FDI is becoming an increasingly important economic link among countries. During the past two decades, the growth of FDI worldwide has been more rapid than that of world output and, more strikingly, of world trade. Several of the APEC nations have been among the fastest-growing hosts of worldwide FDI.[5]

Figure 4-1 shows annual inflows and outflows of FDI for most APEC economies, measured as a ratio to GDP, and Table 4-1 reports average levels of such inflows over time. In Figure 4-1, negative values represent a withdrawal of foreign investment. Experiences in the region are varied. In many of the developing economies there has been a clear underlying increase in inward flows of direct investment over time. Examples include China, Malaysia, Mexico, and Thailand. Such trends presumably reflect a number of factors, including high potential returns caused by long-term shifts in productivity, policies of capital account liberalization, and long-term movements in real exchange rates. By contrast, industrial countries such as Canada, Australia, and New Zealand show no clear trend, presumably reflecting their long tradition of foreign ownership and open capital accounts associated with exploitation of their natural resources.

Flows of FDI can also be compared with portfolio capital flows.[6] Table 4-2 reports data on total flows of net direct investment and portfolio investment during 1990–93 for a number of less developed countries in the APEC region.[7] China was the most important destination for net FDI over this period, followed by Malaysia, Mexico, and Singapore, while Korea and Taiwan Province of China had net outflows. Over the same period, Korea, Mexico, and

---

[1]This section follows the normal practice of using the term FDI to denote the change, in a *flow* sense, in the stock of host-country assets owned by foreigners. The same term is also sometimes used, however, to describe the *stock* of FDI in a host country at a given time.

[2]See Khan and Reinhart (1995) for a discussion of overall capital flows in the APEC region. This section focuses specifically on flows of FDI.

[3]*SNA* (European Union and others, 1993).

[4]Other kinds of data with different definitions are available to measure FDI outflows for some countries because the definition of what constitutes FDI is not standardized across countries. The analysis here (in common with most of the literature) largely uses the standardized *SNA* measure of FDI in the empirical work, thereby ignoring the discrepancy between the underlying economic and statistical concepts.

[5]Ahmad, Roa, and Barnes (1996) contains a detailed discussion of FDI flows in the APEC region.

[6]A fuller discussion of these issues is contained in International Monetary Fund (1995). Khan and Reinhart (1995) have discussed capital flows in the APEC region in more detail, while Bercuson and Koenig (1993) have provided a detailed account of such flows for three members of APEC.

[7]Because these figures refer to net capital inflows, they are not comparable with the data on gross inflows reported in Table 4-1.

Figure 4-1. Ratio of Foreign Direct Investment (FDI) to GDP
(In percent)

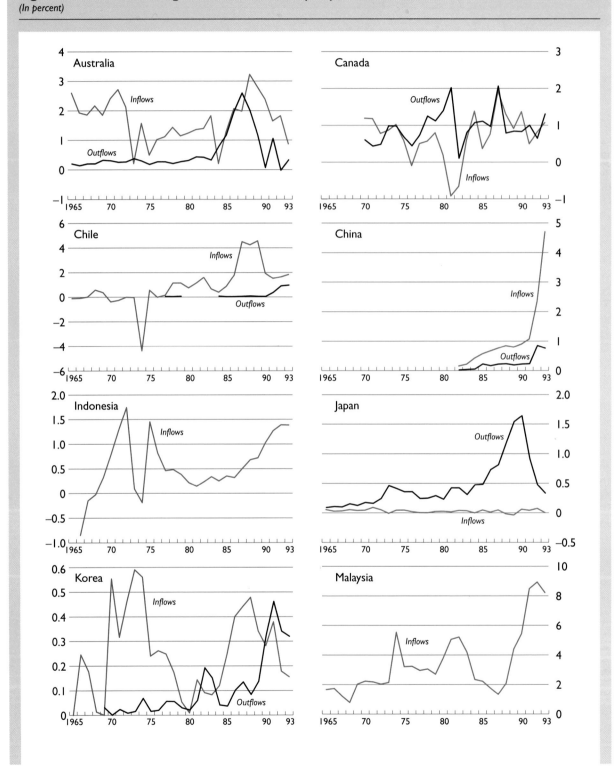

Figure 4-1 *(concluded)*

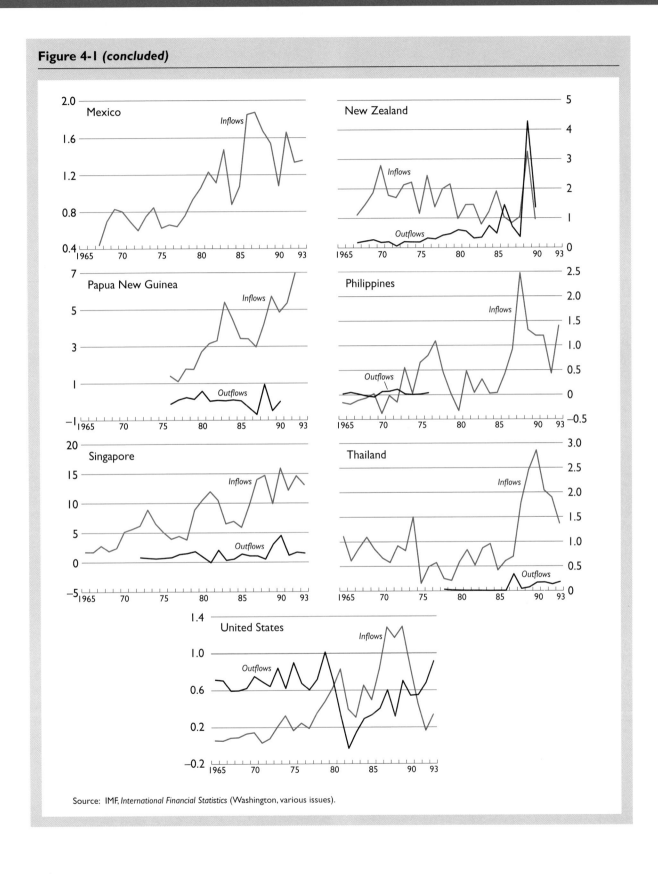

Source: IMF, *International Financial Statistics* (Washington, various issues).

Table 4-1. Ratios of Inward Foreign Direct Investment (FDI) to GDP
(In percent)

APEC Member	1971–80	1981–90	1991–93
Australia	1.3	1.9	1.4
Canada	0.6	0.7	0.8
Chile	–0.1	2.2	1.7
Indonesia	0.7	0.5	1.3
Japan	—	—	—
Korea	0.3	0.3	0.2
Mexico	0.8	1.4	1.4
Malaysia	3.1	3.4	8.5
New Zealand	1.8	1.4	n.a.
Philippines	0.3	0.9	1.0
Singapore	6.4	10.6	13.2
Thailand	0.6	1.2	1.8
United States	0.3	0.8	0.3

Table 4-2. Composition of Net Capital Inflows for Selected APEC Economies, 1990–93
(In billions of U.S. dollars)

APEC Member	Net FDI	Net Portfolio Investment
Chile	1.6	5.0
China	36.6	3.0
Indonesia	6.3	2.7
Korea	–1.4	20.4
Malaysia	11.5	—
Mexico	16.2	23.3
Philippines	1.7	8.6
Singapore	15.4	4.7
Thailand	6.4	31.0
Taiwan Province of China	–7.0	–22.3

Source: IMF, *World Economic Outlook* (various issues).

Thailand were major recipients of portfolio inflows, while Taiwan Province of China experienced a large net outflow. This diversity in experience with respect to different types of capital flows illustrates the disparate nature of the factors underlying alternative types of international capital flows.

Figure 4-1 also shows that there is significant year-to-year variability of FDI inflows around their underlying trends. Inflows to the United States, for example, rose significantly in the mid- to late 1980s but fell in the early 1990s. FDI outflows show a similar level of variability. In the case of Japan, for example, there was a pronounced rise and fall in outflows in the late 1980s and early 1990s.

It is also of interest to look at bilateral outflows of FDI from the United States and Japan, the two most important sources of such investment for the APEC region, to other economies.[8] Figure 4-2 shows these outflows during 1985–94 to six regional groupings, five within APEC plus aggregate non-APEC flows. The APEC regions are the newly industrializing economies (NIEs);[9] other Asian economies;[10] Pacific;[11] other Americas;[12] and Japan or the United

States. Table 4-3 reports the associated cumulated direct investment flows for these regions.

The United States and Japan provided broadly similar aggregate quantities of FDI during the period, with $336 billion coming from the United States and $392 billion from Japan. However, only about one-fourth of aggregate U.S. FDI flows went to other members of APEC, compared with two-thirds in the case of Japan.[13] This largely reflects very different direct bilateral flows between the United States and Japan. Although almost half of the Japanese FDI outflows went to the United States, Japan received only about 3 percent of U.S. outflows. Excluding these direct bilateral connections, cumulated outflows from the United States and Japan to the remaining members of APEC were broadly similar, with the United States investing more in the Americas and Japan holding the edge in Asia and the Pacific.

The dynamic paths of FDI also differ between the United States and Japan. Japanese outflows of FDI to all destinations rose sharply in the late 1980s and then fell equally rapidly in the early 1990s. The rise was stimulated by large current account surpluses, the appreciating yen, and the "bubble economy" in the domestic market, during which the relative abundance of domestic credit combined with the appreciating yen encouraged Japanese firms to invest abroad. As these conditions disappeared in the early

---

[8]The definitions of these bilateral outflows of FDI for the United States and Japan, which come from national sources, are not fully comparable. For example, the data for the United States include currency revaluations and reinvestment, and those for Japan do not.

[9]Hong Kong, Korea, Singapore, and Taiwan Province of China.

[10]Brunei Darussalam, China, Indonesia, Malaysia, the Philippines, and Thailand.

[11]Australia, New Zealand, and Papua New Guinea.

[12]Canada, Chile, and Mexico.

[13]In the case of the United States, the other big recipients were Europe and non-APEC South America.

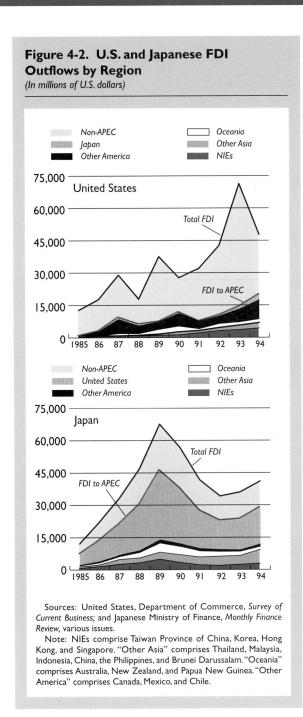

Figure 4-2. U.S. and Japanese FDI Outflows by Region
(In millions of U.S. dollars)

Sources: United States, Department of Commerce, *Survey of Current Business;* and Japanese Ministry of Finance, *Monthly Finance Review,* various issues.

Note: NIEs comprise Taiwan Province of China, Korea, Hong Kong, and Singapore. "Other Asia" comprises Thailand, Malaysia, Indonesia, China, the Philippines, and Brunei Darussalam. "Oceania" comprises Australia, New Zealand, and Papua New Guinea. "Other America" comprises Canada, Mexico, and Chile.

1990s, the earlier upward trend in FDI was reversed. The behavior of U.S. FDI is less easy to characterize, since it is considerably more variable across regions than that of Japan (although some of this may reflect differences in the definition of the data). Direct investment from the United States to APEC as a whole was relatively volatile, with local peaks in 1987, 1990, and 1994.

This points to the need to explore the role of cyclical factors—including temporary exchange rate changes—as determinants of FDI in addition to underlying factors such as productivity trends. Before addressing the issue of how exchange rates affect FDI, however, one must first consider the determinants of FDI more generally. From this viewpoint, the main task to be tackled is to explain why investors need to acquire a controlling interest in a foreign country, rather than simply holding a passive claim (a noncontrolling portfolio share) on that country's output or supplying the market through international trade.

Why FDI Instead of Portfolio Investment?

FDI has two faces: as a method of pursuing higher returns than can be obtained from domestic instruments and as a substitute for or complement to exports and imports.

In trade theory, foreign investment occurs because one country that is relatively short of capital, with abundant labor, would import capital from another country that is relatively abundant in capital. Foreign investment will occur until the returns to capital in different countries are equalized. However, this does not explain why the investment has to be "direct" and take a controlling interest in firms. Obtaining securities—that is, portfolio investment—would suffice to gain access to high-return markets. Major reasons for investment in order to take controlling interest may be that domestic private (capital) markets are inefficient in transforming capital inflows into productive resources, or that managerial know-how is hard to transplant in a different country.

On the other extreme, if market infrastructure (such as the capital markets) or managerial skills are deficient in the host countries, why not export (or import) the products instead of producing goods in the host country? There are several reasons why FDI is favored over trade. Usual explanations include building factories in a country with lower wages when labor mobility is limited, and building assembly lines for products where tariffs and quotas limit imports. In the following paragraphs, these explanations will be elaborated.[14]

The early literature on FDI focused on market size and on the desire to access new markets to extend monopolistic power, to penetrate tightly oligopolistic foreign markets, and to retaliate or preempt for-

---

[14]See Lizondo (1990), Harris and Ravenscraft (1992), Graham and Krugman (1991), and Graham (1995) for reviews of the literature.

Table 4-3. Cumulated Outflows of FDI from the United States and Japan, 1985–92

	United States		Japan	
	In billions of U.S. dollars	In percent of total	In billions of U.S. dollars	In percent of total
Total	336.4	100.0	392.2	100.0
APEC	92.8	27.7	262.0	66.8
Newly industrializing economies[1]	18.5	5.5	25.8	6.6
Other Asia[2]	9.1	2.7	31.3	8.0
Pacific[3]	12.8	3.8	21.9	5.6
Other America[4]	43.5	12.9	8.5	2.2
United States	—	—	174.5	44.5
Japan	9.3	2.8	—	—

Sources: United States, U.S. Department of Commerce, *Survey of Current Business* (various issues); and Japan, Ministry of Finance, *Monthly Finance Review* (various issues).

[1]NIEs: Hong Kong, Korea, Singapore, and Taiwan Province of China.
[2]Brunei Darussalam, China, Indonesia, Malaysia, Philippines, and Thailand.
[3]Australia, New Zealand, and Papua New Guinea.
[4]Canada, Chile, and Mexico.

eign competitors' entry (see, for instance, Kindleberger, 1969, and Caves, 1971). The focus of many multinational firms on the acquisition of leading brands, particularly in the food and consumer product industries, is consistent with this theory. Subsequent research has focused more on firm-specific advantages attributable to greater cost efficiency or product superiority, deriving from economies of scale, multiplant economies, advanced technology and product cycles, or marketing (Vernon, 1974; Dunning, 1974; and Porter, 1986). According to this view, multinationals find it cheaper to expand directly in a foreign country because many of their cost and product advantages rely on internal, indivisible assets, such as organizational and technological know-how. The large share of FDI in industries where research and development and knowledge play a crucial role, such as pharmaceutical and electronics, is consistent with the predictions of this theory. Finally, the need for vertical integration to ensure quality control of production has also received attention.

The recent literature has also considered economies of scale arising from the need to incur marketing costs to promote exports, emphasizing the symbiotic character of FDI and trade (see, for instance, Baldwin and Krugman, 1989, and Dixit, 1989). In the Japanese context, Kojima (1978; see also Kojima and Ozawa, 1984) observed that FDI was "trade-oriented." He hypothesized that Japan invested in countries and sectors that complemented its trading

positions. For example, as some exporting industries of Japan lost competitive advantage because of rising wages, the industries invested abroad. He has also argued that U.S. FDI operated in a rather different manner, acting as a substitute rather than a complement to trade, although this conclusion is not universally shared.[15] These issues are clearly relevant for the APEC region, where Japan and the United States are major contributors of FDI. Others (see, for instance, Errunza and Senbet, 1981) have noted that international operations allow wealth diversification when individual investors are constrained by legal and informational barriers. Related research has emphasized the role of multinational operations in reducing the probability of bankruptcy (Shaked, 1986), and the role of internal liquidity in determining FDI.

Distortions induced by government policies are another major explanation for FDI. Tariffs, quotas, and other import-substituting policies (such as taxes and subsidies) can create conditions under which it is more profitable to produce in—rather than export to—a foreign country (a motivation for FDI often labeled "tariff-jumping"). Preferential tax treatment of foreign investors, specific regulations aimed at favoring foreign investment in specific industries, the use of foreign plants for transfer pricing, and

---

[15]See Lizondo (1990), Section IV.4, for a discussion; see also Ahmad and others (1996).

other policy-induced distortions may also contribute to increasing after-tax returns to FDI and, hence, to raising the level of FDI itself. Thus, observed trends in FDI may reflect changes in these regulations, including changes in the rules on the repatriation of earnings, legal reforms that provide a clearer definition of property rights, political changes that alter the likelihood of nationalization, labor market reforms, and fiscal developments that foster changes in the taxation of capital. Political instability may also be an important factor in certain cases. Again, these factors are clearly relevant for the APEC region.

The host countries generally receive benefits from FDI. In addition to employment opportunities for workers, factories managed by foreign firms are often sources for the learning of managerial skills and the transfer of technology. Many countries prefer foreign companies producing on their soil to imports of the same products. FDI is also generally preferred to portfolio investment by host countries, since direct investment is regarded as a long-run commitment rather than "hot money" that can be withdrawn quickly, often leaving the country's capital market in crisis.

It is also true, however, that host countries often limit possibilities of FDI by banning it altogether in certain industries or capping the share of foreign interest in firms of certain industries. Developing countries often fear, rightly or wrongly, that foreign capital will take over key sectors of the country. Sometimes, restrictions on FDI are also motivated by protection of domestic vested interests. In general, APEC developing countries have become increasingly favorable toward FDI, as can be seen from the upward trend in such investment evident in many countries (see Figure 4-1).

Empirical evidence in support of the determinants of FDI listed above is ample, particularly in support of the link between FDI and economies of scale owing to the ownership of knowledge capital and policy-induced distortions (see Harris and Ravenscraft, 1992, and Klein and Rosengren, 1994, for reviews). These theories are not very helpful, however, in explaining the behavior of FDI over shorter horizons and across countries that exhibit similar characteristics. For instance, foreign acquisitions in the United States fell by 60 percent in 1983, more than doubled between 1986 and 1988, and then fell by 30 percent by 1990 (Harris and Ravenscraft, 1992). The cyclical volatility of FDI is simply too large to be explained by slow-moving structural factors such as those discussed above. To explain the movement of FDI in relation to its historical trend, it is necessary to consider cyclical factors that affect costs and returns to investment. Exchange rates, as main determinants of the relative price of domestic and foreign

goods and production factors, are prime candidates for this task.

Effect of Exchange Rates on FDI

Much of the traditional and modern analysis of the effects of exchange rates on FDI reflects a partial equilibrium perspective, based on the effects of exogenous shifts in real exchange rates on FDI flows. As discussed below, different types of disturbances may produce different links between FDI and exchange rates.

Among the suggested links between the real exchange rate and FDI, the effect of exchange rate changes on asset prices and costs of domestic labor and capital has received the greatest attention. An exchange rate depreciation contributes to FDI by lowering the cost of domestic assets to foreign investors. If the depreciation is perceived to be temporary in real terms (as may be the case for a nominal depreciation that is expected to feed rapidly into local factor and output prices), FDI is likely to include a greater fraction of acquisitions of land and of other existing assets, as foreigners take advantage of bargain prices. Depreciations that are regarded as more permanent in real terms are likely to increase the weight of greenfield investment, through their effect on factor costs, as foreign capital, for instance, seeks to combine with cheaper domestic labor.

A depreciation of the real exchange rate can also lead to an increase in direct investment inflows through its effect on relative wealth across countries (see, for instance, Froot and Stein, 1991, and Klein and Rosengren, 1994). By increasing the relative wealth of foreign firms, a change in the exchange rate can make it relatively easier for those firms to use internal financing, thereby lowering the relative cost of investing. Thus, an exchange rate depreciation would increase foreign firms' wealth relative to domestic firms and spur an FDI inflow.

When one considers the effect of exchange rate changes on FDI coming through its effects on government policy, an opposite effect to that outlined above may be envisioned. To the extent that exchange rate depreciations improve a country's trade balance, they may soften protectionist policies and, with it, reduce the incentive for tariff jumping. Further ambiguities arise when one goes beyond the examination of the effects on FDI of exogenous shocks that cause exchange rates to fall below their long-run trend. Indeed, one must recognize that exchange rates are themselves endogenous variables that respond to a variety of shocks. Depending on the effects of these underlying shocks on the long-run equilibrium exchange rate itself, empirical analysis may uncover quite different linkages between exchange rate changes and FDI flows.

Despite these sources of potential ambiguity, several studies looking largely at industrial countries have provided empirical evidence of a link between exchange rate depreciations and increased FDI inflows—including Cushman (1985, 1987), Caves and Mehra (1986), Culem (1988), Froot and Stein (1991), and Klein and Rosengren (1994). In addition, Harris and Ravenscraft (1991) showed that buyers from strong-currency countries were willing to pay significantly higher premiums than domestic buyers for the acquisition of U.S. assets during 1970–87.

Attention has also been devoted in the literature to the effects of greater exchange rate volatility on FDI. Reasons for greater exchange rate volatility to both stimulate and hinder FDI have been pointed out in the literature. Some authors (for example, Caves and Mehra, 1986) have emphasized the first possibility, based on the view that FDI provides insurance against exchange rate changes by allowing a firm to shift production across countries. From this viewpoint, greater exchange rate uncertainty is likely to cause more FDI (see also Aizenman, 1994, for a discussion of these issues). In contrast, the view that exchange rate volatility may reduce FDI has been emphasized by those noting the irreversible nature of FDI (see Dixit, 1989), which causes investors to be wary of potential exchange rate reversals when undertaking a foreign investment project that involves an unrecoverable outlay. This particular channel is more likely to apply when investment is of a greenfield nature, or with certain types of investment undertaken in support of trade (for example, the cost of setting up a foreign plant, of developing a distribution network, or of establishing brand recognition). It has also been noted that some of the diversification motives applying to portfolio investment may extend to FDI (see Black, 1977). Exchange rate volatility should reduce portfolio investment and, by similarity (or if FDI remains in broadly constant proportion to portfolio investment), also FDI. This presumption is subject to qualifications, however. Countries whose exchange rates are negatively correlated with global returns to capital (for instance, oil-exporting countries), may actually benefit from their role as portfolio hedges. An increase in these countries' exchange rate volatility may actually raise their FDI inflows on diversification grounds.

Empirical evidence on the link between exchange rate volatility and FDI is limited but tends to favor a positive link between exchange rate volatility and FDI inflows (see, for instance, Cushman, 1985, and Caves and Mehra, 1986). In response to greater exchange rate risk, multinationals appear to reduce exports to a foreign country but to offset this somewhat by increasing capital inputs and production in the country.

Empirical Evidence for the APEC Region

To investigate the links between FDI inflows and medium-term changes in the real exchange rate, we present regression results using annual data drawn from the APEC economies.[16] The starting date of this empirical study is 1974, which marked the beginning of the current flexible exchange rate regime. It is well documented that this change in the nominal exchange rate regime also led to a significant change in the behavior of real exchange rates. The dependent variable in these regressions is the ratio of direct investment inflows (the sum of lines 45, 46, and 47 in the IMF's *Balance of Payments Statistics Yearbook*) to host-country GDP. Data on investment outflows were not used because they were not available for all economies.

The preceding discussion implies that the relationship between changes in the real exchange rate and direct investment inflows is ambiguous. A real depreciation may stimulate such flows by increasing the relative wealth of potential investors and by lowering costs in the host country. An appreciation of the exchange rate can be associated with increased FDI if the appreciation reflects a general surge in capital flows or if it increases protectionist pressures. The regression results will only be able to identify the general relationship between FDI and changes in the exchange rate. More disaggregated data on direct investment and other factors would be needed to help further distinguish among these potential channels.

The regressions relate the ratio of inflows of FDI to the level of the real exchange rate. To isolate the effect of the real exchange rate from some other possible factors that might be correlated with direct investment, two other independent variables were included in the initial regressions. The first was the growth of real output in the host country (measured as the change in the logarithm of real GDP from the previous year to the current year). The second was a time trend, so as to control for secular changes in inward FDI relative to GDP. Because the trend was found to be insignificant in most regressions, it was only included in the final specification when it was statistically significant.

Two specifications of the regressions are reported, and they differ according to the type of real ex-

---

[16]More general empirical analyses of FDI in Asia, and of its relationship to trade and growth, are contained in Eaton and Tamura (1994, 1996).

Table 4-4. Results from FDI Regressions Using Real Effective Exchange Rates

(FDI/GDP)$_t$ = α + β Δlog(Y_t) + Ψ log(E_t)

APEC Member	Growth in GDP	Real Effective Exchange Rate	R^2	Adjusted for Autocorrelation
Panel of all countries	0.061*	−0.024**	0.79	No
Australia	−0.087	−0.013	0.17	Yes
Canada	0.064	−0.021	0.13	Yes
Chile	−0.026	−0.042**	0.58	No
Indonesia	−0.041	−0.006	0.10	Yes
Japan	−0.004	−0.001*	0.15	No
Korea	0.014	−0.003	0.43	Yes
Mexico	−0.022	−0.009	0.61	Yes
Malaysia	0.034	−0.030	0.20	Yes
Philippines	0.047*	−0.032**	0.62	No
Singapore	0.323	−0.030	0.61	Yes
Thailand	0.101	0.027	0.19	Yes
United States	0.023	−0.009	0.10	Yes

Note: One and two asterisks indicate that the coefficient is significant at the 5 and 1 percent levels, respectively. Time trends were included in the regressions for Japan, Mexico, and Singapore.

change rate variable used. The regressions in Table 4-4 use the multilateral effective real exchange rate for each country. This variable has the advantage of representing the real exchange rate of the host country with respect to a broad range of other countries. The shortcoming of the multilateral effective real exchange rate is that the weights used to construct it are based on trade flows rather than on capital flows. Therefore, in Table 4-5 results are presented that used two separate bilateral real exchange rates, those against the United States and Japan, the major sources of direct investment for other APEC economies. Estimation was generally by ordinary least squares; however, in those cases where the residuals appeared to be significantly serially correlated, an autocorrelation adjustment was used, as indicated in the final columns of the tables. Finally, a panel regression was run in which the data from all of the available countries were included in a single specification (without an autocorrelation adjustment or a time trend). The results from these regressions can be thought of as representing evidence on the average behavior across the whole sample of countries.

The regression results in Table 4-4 indicate that depreciations of the multilateral real exchange rate are generally associated with an increase in inward direct investment relative to GDP (all real exchange rate variables were defined such that an increase represents an appreciation). The coefficient on the real effective exchange rate is negative in the panel regression and in 11 of the 12 regressions for individual economies, although it is significant at conventional levels only in the panel regression and in 3 of the individual regressions. The coefficient of −0.024 in the panel regression indicates that for every 1 percent appreciation in the real effective exchange rate, FDI is lowered by 0.024 percentage point of GDP. Although this may appear small, it has to be gauged against both the relatively large movements in real effective exchange rates across economies and the low ratios of investment inflows as a percentage of output. For example, a 10 percent appreciation in the real effective exchange rate would lower FDI by almost ¼ of 1 percent of GDP, which is a significant proportion of the underlying inflows into many APEC economies (see Table 4-1).

The exchange rate coefficients for individual economies are generally similar in magnitude to the panel results, except in the case of Japan, where the coefficient is significantly lower. This presumably reflects the relatively low ratio of inward FDI in Japan. The coefficients for income growth are generally small, insignificant, and of variable sign, implying a weak link between growth and FDI (although the panel regression has a significant positive coefficient).[17]

---

[17]Because the dependent variable is measured as a ratio to nominal GDP, which includes real GDP as one of its components, the level of real GDP is also implicitly included in the regression.

Table 4-5. Results from FDI Regressions Using Real Bilateral Exchange Rates
$(FDI/GDP)_t = \alpha + \beta \Delta \log(Y_t) + \Psi_1 \log(E_{USt}) + \Psi_2 \log(E_{JAt})$

APEC Member	Growth of Real GDP	U.S. Real Exchange Rate	Japanese Real Exchange Rate	R^2	Adjusted for Autocorrelation
Panel of all countries	0.051	0.007	−0.023**	0.80	No
Australia	−0.071	0.016	−0.019**	0.34	No
Canada	0.099	0.023	−0.018**	0.35	No
Chile	−0.057	0.010	−0.045	0.42	Yes
Indonesia	0.058	0.009	−0.011	0.13	Yes
Japan	−0.005	−0.000	...	0.15	No
Korea	0.013	−0.002	−0.001	0.41	Yes
Mexico	−0.034	0.003	−0.010**	0.67	No
Malaysia	0.040	−0.059	0.012	0.21	Yes
Philippines	0.068*	−0.016	−0.011	0.63	No
Singapore	0.346	0.028	−0.011	0.68	No
Thailand	0.159	0.015	0.017	0.45	Yes
United States	0.014	...	−0.006	0.11	Yes

Note: One and two asterisks indicate that the coefficient is significant at the 5 and 1 percent level, respectively. Time trends were included in the regressions for Singapore and Thailand.

Table 4-5 presents results from the same basic regression, but where the real effective exchange rate for each host country was replaced by two bilateral real exchange rates, those with respect to the United States and with respect to Japan. (The regressions for Japan and the United States, of course, include only one bilateral real exchange rate.) The results from these regressions confirm many of those found in the previous regressions using effective exchange rates. The coefficients on the growth of real GDP are generally insignificant, while there appears to be a significant negative relationship between real exchange rates and FDI. This negative relationship is clear in the case of the real exchange rate with respect to Japan, where both the panel regression and all but one of the individual regressions have negative coefficients, and the coefficient estimate in the panel regression is highly significant. The results for bilateral rates with respect to the United States, however, show little pattern. None of the regression coefficients is significantly different from zero, and many of them, including that in the panel regression, are positively signed.

This last result suggests a potential difference in the behavior of FDI from the United States and from Japan with respect to the exchange rate. To investigate this possibility further, data on bilateral flows of FDI from the United States and Japan to eight developing countries in the APEC region (Chile, Korea, Indonesia, Mexico, Malaysia, Philippines, Singapore, and Thailand) were col-

lected.[18] Unfortunately, the longest period for which consistent data could be obtained was 1980–93, which is rather too short for reliable estimation of regressions for individual economies. Instead, panel regressions were estimated, as reported below, relating the ratio of the bilateral flow of U.S. (Japanese) FDI to the GDP of the recipient country to the growth of real GDP in the host country (ΔY), and to the bilateral real exchange rate (E) for the U.S. dollar (yen):[19]

$$(FDI_{US}/GDP)_t = 0.052^{**}\Delta Y_t + .002E_{USt-1},$$
$$R^2 = 0.12$$

$$(FDI_{JA}/GDP)_t = 0.022\Delta Y_t - .004^*E_{JAt-1},$$
$$R^2 = 0.11.$$

These regressions also indicate a difference in behavior between FDI coming from Japan and the United States. The coefficient on the real bilateral exchange rate in the panel regression for FDI from Japan was −0.004 and significant at the 5 percent level (although somewhat smaller than the corresponding coefficient on the corresponding real exchange rate in the panel regression reported in Table

---

[18]These data came from OECD sources and, hence, are not necessarily compatible with the multilateral IMF data used in the previous regressions.

[19]Note that the lagged exchange rate was used in these regressions because it appeared to work better than the contemporaneous value.

4-5), while that on the bilateral real exchange rate in the panel regression for FDI from the United States was 0.002 and insignificant. Another contrast is that real GDP growth in the recipient country appears to matter for U.S. FDI flows but not for their Japanese counterpart.

Concluding Perspectives

Most of the factors affecting FDI flows are secular, as befits an activity that is long term by nature. This does not mean, however, that short-term factors have no influence in such decisions. In particular, a depreciation of the real exchange rate may stimulate inflows of direct investment by increasing the relative wealth of the investor and reducing the costs of domestic assets and factors of production. In contrast, an appreciation of the real exchange rate could also be associated with increased FDI if the appreciation reflects the impact of a general surge in capital flows or if it decreases protectionist pressures.

Earlier empirical work has found that capital inflows are generally associated with exchange rate depreciations, which is consistent with the idea that the wealth and cost channels predominate. The empirical work reported here for countries in the APEC region confirms this finding. There is, however, some evidence that foreign investment flows from the two largest economies in the region behave somewhat differently in this regard, with investment from the United States being less dependent on changes in the real exchange rate than the corresponding flows from Japan.[20] This difference might indicate that the factors driving U.S. and Japanese FDI are rather different, although more work would be required to sustain such a conclusion.

References

Ahmad, Ashfaq, P. Someshwar Roa, and Colleen Barnes, 1996, "Foreign Direct Investment and APEC Economic Integration," Working Paper 8 (Ottawa: Industry Canada, February).

Aizenman, Joshua, 1994, "Monetary and Real Shocks, Productive Capacity, and Exchange Rate Regimes," *Economica*, Vol. 61 (November), pp. 407–34.

---

[20]This may be due in part to the nature of the data. In particular, some of the FDI inflows from the United States in the past two decades may reflect reinvestment of income earned on, or appreciation in the value of, investments undertaken in the 1950s and 1960s; such reinvestment or appreciation is counted as FDI inflows. By contrast, Japanese investments in the regions are newer, and the timing of the initial investment may have been more sensitive to exchange rate fluctuations. At this point, however, this observation remains a conjecture.

Baldwin, Richard, and Paul R. Krugman, 1989, "Persistent Trade Effects of Large Exchange Rate Shocks," *Quarterly Journal of Economics*, Vol. 104 (November), pp. 635–54.

Bercuson, Kenneth B., and Linda M. Koenig, 1993, "The Recent Surge in Capital Inflows to Three ASEAN Countries: Causes and Macroeconomic Impact," Occasional Paper No. 15 (Kuala Lumpur: South East Asian Central Banks (SEACEN) Research and Training Center).

Black, Stanley W., 1977, *Floating Exchange Rates and National Economic Policy* (New Haven, Conn.: Yale University Press).

Caves, Richard E., 1971, "International Corporations: The Industrial Economics of Foreign Investment," *Economica*, Vol. 38 (February), pp. 1–27.

Caves, R.E., and Sanjeev Mehra, 1986, "Entry of Foreign Multinationals into U.S. Manufacturing Industries," in *Competition in Global Industries*, ed. by Michael E. Porter (Boston, Mass.: Harvard Business School Press).

Culem, Claudy G., 1988, "The Locational Determinants of Foreign Direct Investments Among Industrialized Countries," *European Economic Review*, Vol. 32 (April), pp. 885–904.

Cushman, David O., 1985, "Real Exchange Rate Risk, Expectations, and the Level of Foreign Direct Investment," *Review of Economics and Statistics*, Vol. 67 (May), pp. 297–308.

———, 1987, "The Effects of Real Wages and Labor Productivity on Foreign Direct Investment," *Southern Economics Journal*, Vol. 54 (July), pp. 174–85.

Dixit, Avinash, 1989, "Hysteresis, Import Penetration, and Exchange Rate Pass-Through," *Quarterly Journal of Economics*, Vol. 104 (May), pp. 205–28.

Dunning, J., 1974, "The Distinctive Nature of the Multinational Enterprise," in *Economic Analysis and the Multinational Enterprise*, ed. by John H. Dunning (London: Allen and Unwin).

Eaton, Jonathan, and Akiko Tamura, 1994, "Bilateralism and Regionalism in Japanese and U.S. Trade and Direct Foreign Investment Patterns," *Journal of Japanese and International Economics*, Vol. 8 (December), pp. 478–510.

———, 1996, "Japanese and U.S. Exports and Investment as Conduits of Growth," in *Financial Deregulation and Integration in East Asia*, ed. by Takatoshi Ito and Anne Krueger (Chicago: University of Chicago Press).

Errunza, V., and Senbet, L., 1981, "The Effects of International Operations on the Market Value of the Firm: Theory and Evidence," *Journal of Finance*, Vol. 36, pp. 401–17.

European Union, International Monetary Fund, Organization for Economic Cooperation and Development, United Nations, and World Bank, 1993, *System of National Accounts 1993* (Brussels/Luxembourg, New York, Paris, Washington).

Froot, Kenneth, 1991, "Japanese Foreign Direct Investment," NBER Working Paper 3737 (Cambridge, Mass.: National Bureau of Economic Research).

Froot, Kenneth, and J. Stein, 1991, "Exchange Rates and Foreign Investment: An Imperfect Capital Markets

Approach," *Quarterly Journal of Economics*, Vol. 106 (November), pp. 1191–1217.

Graham, Edward M., 1995, "Foreign Direct Investment in the World Economy," IMF Working Paper 95/59 (Washington: International Monetary Fund).

Graham, Edward M., and Paul R. Krugman, 1991, *Foreign Direct Investment in the United States*, 2nd ed. (Washington: Institute for International Economics).

Harris, Robert S., and David J. Ravenscraft, 1991, "The Role of Acquisitions in Foreign Direct Investment: Evidence from the U.S. Stock Market," *Journal of Finance*, Vol. 46 (July), pp. 825–44.

———, 1992, "Foreign Takeovers," in *The New Palgrave Dictionary of Money and Finance*, ed. by Peter Newman, Murray Milgate, and John Eatwell (New York: Stockton), pp. 174–78.

International Monetary Fund, 1995, *International Capital Markets: Developments, Prospects, and Policy Issues*, World Economic and Financial Surveys (Washington).

Kester, W.C., 1991, *Japanese Takeovers: The Global Contest for Corporate Control* (Boston, Mass.: Harvard Business School Press).

Khan, Mohsin S., and Carmen M. Reinhart, eds., 1995, *Capital Flows in the APEC Region*, Occasional Paper 122 (Washington: International Monetary Fund, March).

Kindleberger, Charles P., 1969, *American Business Abroad: Six Lectures on Direct Investment* (New Haven, Conn.: Yale University Press).

Klein, Michael W., and Eric Rosengren, 1994, "The Real Exchange Rate and Foreign Direct Investment in the United States," *Journal of International Economics*, Vol. 36 (May), pp. 373–89.

Kojima, Kiyoshi, 1978, *Direct Foreign Investment* (London: Croom Helm).

Kojima, Kiyoshi, and Terutomo Ozawa, 1984, "Micro- and Macroeconomic Models of Direct Foreign Investment: Toward a Synthesis," *Hitotsubashi Journal of Economics*, Vol. 25 (June), pp. 1–20.

Lizondo, José Saul, 1990, "Foreign Direct Investment," IMF Working Paper 90/63 (Washington: International Monetary Fund).

Porter, Michael E., 1986, *Competition in Global Industries* (Boston, Mass.: Harvard Business School Press).

Shaked, Israel, 1986, "Are Multinational Corporations Safer?" *Journal of International Business Studies*, Vol. 17 (Spring), pp. 83–106.

Vernon, R., 1974, "The Location of Economic Activity," in *Economic Analysis and the Multinational Enterprise*, ed. by John H. Dunning (London: Allen and Unwin).

Recent Occasional Papers of the International Monetary Fund

145. Exchange Rate Movements and Their Impact on Trade and Investment in the APEC Region, by Takatoshi Ito, Peter Isard, Steven Symansky, and Tamim Bayoumi. 1996.

144. National Bank of Poland: The Road to Indirect Instruments, by Piero Ugolini. 1996.

143. Adjustment for Growth: The African Experience, by Michael T. Hadjimichael, Michael Nowak, Robert Sharer, and Amor Tahari. 1996.

142. Quasi-Fiscal Operations of Public Financial Institutions, by G.A. Mackenzie and Peter Stella. 1996.

141. Monetary and Exchange System Reforms in China: An Experiment in Gradualism, by Hassanali Mehran, Marc Quintyn, Tom Nordman, and Bernard Laurens. 1996.

140. Government Reform in New Zealand, by Graham C. Scott. 1996.

139. Reinvigorating Growth in Developing Countries: Lessons from Adjustment Policies in Eight Economies, by David Goldsbrough, Sharmini Coorey, Louis Dicks-Mireaux, Balazs Horvath, Kalpana Kochhar, Mauro Mecagni, Erik Offerdal, and Jianping Zhou. 1996.

138. Aftermath of the CFA Franc Devaluation, by Jean A.P. Clément, with Johannes Mueller, Stéphane Cossé, and Jean Le Dem. 1996.

137. The Lao People's Democratic Republic: Systemic Transformation and Adjustment, edited by Ichiro Otani and Chi Do Pham. 1996.

136. Jordan: Strategy for Adjustment and Growth, edited by Edouard Maciejewski and Ahsan Mansur. 1996.

135. Vietnam: Transition to a Market Economy, by John R. Dodsworth, Erich Spitäller, Michael Braulke, Keon Hyok Lee, Kenneth Miranda, Christian Mulder, Hisanobu Shishido, and Krishna Srinivasan. 1996.

134. India: Economic Reform and Growth, by Ajai Chopra, Charles Collyns, Richard Hemming, and Karen Parker with Woosik Chu and Oliver Fratzscher. 1995.

133. Policy Experiences and Issues in the Baltics, Russia, and Other Countries of the Former Soviet Union, edited by Daniel A. Citrin and Ashok K. Lahiri. 1995.

132. Financial Fragilities in Latin America: The 1980s and 1990s, by Liliana Rojas-Suárez and Steven R. Weisbrod. 1995.

131. Capital Account Convertibility: Review of Experience and Implications for IMF Policies, by staff teams headed by Peter J. Quirk and Owen Evans. 1995.

130. Challenges to the Swedish Welfare State, by Desmond Lachman, Adam Bennett, John H. Green, Robert Hagemann, and Ramana Ramaswamy. 1995.

129. IMF Conditionality: Experience Under Stand-By and Extended Arrangements. Part II: Background Papers. Susan Schadler, Editor, with Adam Bennett, Maria Carkovic, Louis Dicks-Mireaux, Mauro Mecagni, James H.J. Morsink, and Miguel A. Savastano. 1995.

128. IMF Conditionality: Experience Under Stand-By and Extended Arrangements. Part I: Key Issues and Findings, by Susan Schadler, Adam Bennett, Maria Carkovic, Louis Dicks-Mireaux, Mauro Mecagni, James H.J. Morsink, and Miguel A. Savastano. 1995.

127. Road Maps of the Transition: The Baltics, the Czech Republic, Hungary, and Russia, by Biswajit Banerjee, Vincent Koen, Thomas Krueger, Mark S. Lutz, Michael Marrese, and Tapio O. Saavalainen 1995.

126. The Adoption of Indirect Instruments of Monetary Policy, by a staff team headed by William E. Alexander, Tomás J.T. Baliño, and Charles Enoch. 1995.

125. United Germany: The First Five Years—Performance and Policy Issues, by Robert Corker, Robert A. Feldman, Karl Habermeier, Hari Vittas, and Tessa van der Willigen. 1995.

124. Saving Behavior and the Asset Price "Bubble" in Japan: Analytical Studies, edited by Ulrich Baumgartner and Guy Meredith. 1995.

123. Comprehensive Tax Reform: The Colombian Experience, edited by Parthasarathi Shome. 1995.

122. Capital Flows in the APEC Region, edited by Mohsin S. Khan and Carmen M. Reinhart. 1995.

121. Uganda: Adjustment with Growth, 1987–94, by Robert L. Sharer, Hema R. De Zoysa, and Calvin A. McDonald. 1995.

120. Economic Dislocation and Recovery in Lebanon, by Sena Eken, Paul Cashin, S. Nuri Erbas, Jose Martelino, and Adnan Mazarei. 1995.

119. Singapore: A Case Study in Rapid Development, edited by Kenneth Bercuson with a staff team comprising Robert G. Carling, Aasim M. Husain, Thomas Rumbaugh, and Rachel van Elkan. 1995.

118. Sub-Saharan Africa: Growth, Savings, and Investment, by Michael T. Hadjimichael, Dhaneshwar Ghura, Martin Mühleisen, Roger Nord, and E. Murat Uçer. 1995.

117. Resilience and Growth Through Sustained Adjustment: The Moroccan Experience, by Saleh M. Nsouli, Sena Eken, Klaus Enders, Van-Can Thai, Jörg Decressin, and Filippo Cartiglia, with Janet Bungay. 1995.

116. Improving the International Monetary System: Constraints and Possibilities, by Michael Mussa, Morris Goldstein, Peter B. Clark, Donald J. Mathieson, and Tamim Bayoumi. 1994.

115. Exchange Rates and Economic Fundamentals: A Framework for Analysis, by Peter B. Clark, Leonardo Bartolini, Tamim Bayoumi, and Steven Symansky. 1994.

114. Economic Reform in China: A New Phase, by Wanda Tseng, Hoe Ee Khor, Kalpana Kochhar, Dubravko Mihaljek, and David Burton. 1994.

113. Poland: The Path to a Market Economy, by Liam P. Ebrill, Ajai Chopra, Charalambos Christofides, Paul Mylonas, Inci Otker, and Gerd Schwartz. 1994.

112. The Behavior of Non-Oil Commodity Prices, by Eduardo Borensztein, Mohsin S. Khan, Carmen M. Reinhart, and Peter Wickham. 1994.

111. The Russian Federation in Transition: External Developments, by Benedicte Vibe Christensen. 1994.

110. Limiting Central Bank Credit to the Government: Theory and Practice, by Carlo Cottarelli. 1993.

109. The Path to Convertibility and Growth: The Tunisian Experience, by Saleh M. Nsouli, Sena Eken, Paul Duran, Gerwin Bell, and Zühtü Yücelik. 1993.

108. Recent Experiences with Surges in Capital Inflows, by Susan Schadler, Maria Carkovic, Adam Bennett, and Robert Kahn. 1993.

107. China at the Threshold of a Market Economy, by Michael W. Bell, Hoe Ee Khor, and Kalpana Kochhar, with Jun Ma, Simon N'guiamba, and Rajiv Lall. 1993.

106. Economic Adjustment in Low-Income Countries: Experience Under the Enhanced Structural Adjustment Facility, by Susan Schadler, Franek Rozwadowski, Siddharth Tiwari, and David O. Robinson. 1993.

105. The Structure and Operation of the World Gold Market, by Gary O'Callaghan. 1993.

104. Price Liberalization in Russia: Behavior of Prices, Household Incomes, and Consumption During the First Year, by Vincent Koen and Steven Phillips. 1993.

103. Liberalization of the Capital Account: Experiences and Issues, by Donald J. Mathieson and Liliana Rojas-Suárez. 1993.

102. Financial Sector Reforms and Exchange Arrangements in Eastern Europe. Part I: Financial Markets and Intermediation, by Guillermo A. Calvo and Manmohan S. Kumar. Part II: Exchange Arrangements of Previously Centrally Planned Economies, by Eduardo Borensztein and Paul R. Masson. 1993.

101. Spain: Converging with the European Community, by Michel Galy, Gonzalo Pastor, and Thierry Pujol. 1993.

100. The Gambia: Economic Adjustment in a Small Open Economy, by Michael T. Hadjimichael, Thomas Rumbaugh, and Eric Verreydt. 1992.

Note: For information on the title and availability of Occasional Papers not listed, please consult the IMF Publications Catalog or contact IMF Publication Services.